Compelling Conversations

Connecting Leadership
to Student Achievement

Compelling Conversations

Connecting Leadership
to Student Achievement

THOMASINA DEPINTO PIERCY

EDITED BY
SARAH CURTIS

A CO-PUBLICATION OF

LEAD+
LEARN
PRESS

American Association of
School Administrators

Lead + Learn Press
317 Inverness Way South, Suite 150
Englewood, CO 80112
Phone (866) 399-6019 or (303) 504-9312 ▪ Fax (303) 504-9417
www.LeadandLearn.com

Library of Congress Cataloging-in-Publication Data
Piercy, Thomasina, 1950–
    Compelling conversations : connecting leadership to achievement / Thomasina Piercy.
        p. cm.
    Includes bibliographical references.
    ISBN 1-933196-25-4
      1. Educational leadership—United States. 2. Academic achievement—United States. 3. Educational accountability—United States I. Title.

LB2805.P585 2006
379.1'58—dc22   2005057209

ISBN 978-1-933196-25-1

Printed in the United States of America

14 13 12 11 10 09   03 04 05 06 07 08

Contents

CHAPTER 2   **Conversations: The Shared Approach to Accountability**   55

> ESSENTIAL QUESTION: How can individual Compelling Conversations with teachers contribute to measurable Data Team goals?
>
> Explores the vital connection between data from individual Compelling Conversations, accountability resulting from the work of Data Teams, and shared accountability.

CHAPTER 3   **Conversations: A Collaborative Model for Instruction**   85

> ESSENTIAL QUESTION: How can the themes revealed in Compelling Conversations and the data patterns that emerge redefine beliefs, roles, and instructional models?
>
> Shows how student- and team-specific data lead to a collaborative culture and support for achieving standards. Describes Invisible Excellence and the double-instructed reading process.

     ESSENTIAL QUESTION: How can Compelling Conversations establish a culture for a professional learning community that sustains achievement and future change?

     Investigates how multiple levels of communication shift the roles of principals and school leaders, teachers, and school specialists. Shows how closing the void between teacher quality and student progress, through the role of a contributing leader, results in increased teacher leadership capacity.

Foreword

EING OF A CERTAIN AGE, I remember the old Johnny Carson television show, *Who(m) Do You Trust?* (Hint to readers who are unfamiliar with the show: it was broadcast in black and white!) Although the show is long gone, its title could well be the subtitle for this book, because at its core, *Compelling Conversations* is about trust. Thomasina Piercy describes the creation of a school culture in which teachers are trusted as professionals—where their judgments lie at the heart of critical conversations about learning and their actions are trusted to make a difference. *Compelling Conversations* also makes the case for trusting data: not simply the annual "snapshot" scores offered by an external test, but the data provided by a continuous stream of moment-in-time images from ongoing assessments. Along the way, readers come to trust the perceptions and prescriptions of Dr. Piercy, a veteran teacher and administrator, who marries her palpable caring about kids with a hard-nosed practicality born of experience. Fundamentally, the book places its trust in the capacity of educators to make a difference for *every* learner—a belief in human capabilities that trumps the passivity and fatalism resident in too many schools.

An alternative subtitle comes to mind: *No Child Left Behind.* Nowadays, this title wouldn't make it past the editor's desk. To many of today's educators, these words represent the politicization of their world and evoke the unrelenting accountability pressures associated with high-stakes testing. Yet, if one can disassociate the phrase from its political connection, "no child left behind" offers an apt description of *Compelling Conversations.* At its most basic level, the book *acts* on the phrase without becoming mired in the politics associated with the law that was so named. Indeed, the importance of this book lies in its detailed description of a process for translating a catch phrase (that many see as idealistic rhetoric or political hyperbole) into a practical system for realizing the intent inherent in that phrase.

The basic approach described in the book borders on the simplistic: set clear goals; find out where you are and "map backward" to determine what you have to do to close the gap; monitor frequently and adjust when you find yourself off course; and focus on individuals, not averages. Well, of course! Every effective coach and extracurricular sponsor knows that. Yet this simple clarity is all too easily eroded in the whirlwind of school and the everpresent "toos": too many students, too little planning time, too much content to cover, too little parental support, too much testing. Dr. Piercy acknowledges the realities (the opening of this book alludes to the leaky pipes in her time-worn school building), while refusing to allow all the "yes, buts" to compromise her vision and derail the needed actions.

It's in the details that *Compelling Conversations* offers a refreshing and compelling voice amidst the school-reform cacophony. From her years of "walking the talk" as a teacher and administrator, Thommie Piercy has developed a systematic approach for focusing the energy of a school on every child's growth as a learner. As a transformative educational leader, she understands that meaningful and lasting school reform comes about by attending to the school culture, not through mandates. She further recognizes that conversations lie at the heart of a school's culture and thus serve as the nexus of school improvement. She illustrates how a leader "leads for learning" by structuring these conversations.

Compelling Conversations functions like MapQuest. It provides a broad vision of the landscape to guide the overall journey, while progressively zooming in to provide street-by-street directions to willing travelers. Though the book is not formulaic, its directions are sufficiently detailed to enable emulation by energetic and focused educational leaders. The inclusion of practical organizers, forms, and samples renders the invisible visible, and the abstract tangible. Her insertion of the voices of teachers and students personalizes the theoretical.

Piercy's writing style defies genre typecasting, refreshingly blending visionary, lyrical language with research citations. Her perspective integrates the intellectual rigor of an academic with the sensitivity of an artist, while her actions marry the no-nonsense demeanor of a veteran educator with the caring of a therapist.

Given the current educational fixation on "results," along with dozens of recent books offering "the answer," skeptical practitioners have the right to demur at the advice of ivory-tower academics and "in-and-out" consultants. Nevertheless, anyone who doubts the credibility of and wise counsel in this book runs the risk of being labeled a cynic. Thomasina Piercy is believable. She has spent years refining this approach, and evidence of its effectiveness comes from hard data (i.e., test scores) as well as the testimonials of teachers and the learning of students. I trust that you, your staff, and your learners will similarly benefit from the messages of this compelling book.

:: JAY McTIGHE ::

Preface

C AN A BULLDOZER OF FEDERAL LEGISLATION, using the blade of state financial rewards, change processes weighted down by generations of established tradition? After all, the National Assessment of Educational Progress (NAEP) has provided public education feedback that the numbers of students performing proficiently and above has not improved for more than 20 years! The NAEP, the "federal government's most important and most respected measure of U.S. schools" (Public Education Network, 2004, p. 4), indicated a stagnant uptick of only 4 points from 1971 to 1999. Additionally, the at-risk students who were targeted—and for whom schools and districts received substantial financial support—made at best minimal gains.

Currently, "the federal government is rewriting the NAEP so that the tests will reflect a greater emphasis on basic skills instead of their current balance between basic and higher-order skills. By squeezing out critical thinking skills, these actions put the cognitive development of our students at risk" (Wenglinsky, 2004, p. 35). How much longer can we educators continue to scratch our heads, asking questions such as, "So now the way to increase student learning is to make the test easier?" In addition, there are the frustrations created by the requirements of the No Child Left Behind act (NCLB), mandating that all students make adequate yearly progress (AYP). As a practicing principal, I am living your frustrations daily while breathing the same air of hope.

Compelling Conversations details a process to improve student achievement, assuring that every child has access to the same high quality of education and meets the same standards by establishing the control for change directly at the school level. Standards allow every student to move toward success (Reeves, 2004). High-stakes assessments provide data developed by accountability experts—but if the data are not timely or informative, they cannot help increase learning. Elementary and middle school principals and school leaders who look inside their own buildings for the real experts will find them in abundance: their teachers! Believing in your teachers translates directly into believing in your students. A new era is here, and it is time for principals and school leaders to inhabit the present reality with honesty. Schools are filled with hundreds of young lives needing timeless skills to face unimaginable futures; leading these schools by following tired, outdated models, equipped only with end-of-year state assessments, is just wrong. These structures were only minimally successful two decades ago, and are even less effective now.

Today, Compelling Conversations tap into the voice of the culture—a voice of believing. Compelling Conversations are centered on increasing communication between teachers and school leaders about expectations for standards to be achieved by all students. Wenglinsky (2004, p. 35) explains, "Education leaders should embrace the notion of being held accountable for the achievement of their students, but demand autonomy in how to improve that achievement."

The current field of education is divided into separate empires of expertise related to school improvement: accountability, assessment, content strategies, and professional communities. As if principals could write a dissertation daily on their way to work, principals are continuously bombarded with excellent conceptual frameworks within which they must maneuver to generate success. During days filled with the silent screams of non-English-speaking children in crisis, parental requests for immediate attention, and classrooms increasingly assigned to noncertified teachers, *Compelling Conversations* helps principals by assimilating and refocusing the current array of insightful concepts about school improvement. Successful student performance on school, district, and state assessments of content standards is possible when school communities begin interconnected conversations to understand students' progress, resulting in "student-centered accountability" (Reeves, 2004).

My purpose in writing this book is to highlight the essential role of conversations between school leaders and teachers in decisions related to student achievement. The synergy created during Compelling Conversations has the potential to shift traditional expectations for student standards, teacher and administrative roles, and attitudes about assessment and accountability.

Chapter 1 describes the powerful relationship between Compelling Conversations and student achievement, and supports these ideas with triangulated data. It establishes the framework for principals and school leaders to begin incorporating Compelling Conversations with every teacher as a process for school improvement.

It is important to keep in mind that multiple variables affect student performance, as in all dynamic organizations. We do not claim that Compelling Conversations are solely responsible for increases in student achievement, but the data are themselves compelling. Throughout, you will find data and examples focused on reading, which is where we started using Compelling Conversations;

however, given the good results gained by middle and elementary schools in other districts and states in the areas of reading and math, we believe the Compelling Conversations process can be fruitfully applied to any content area.

Chapter 2 explains the principles for continuing the conversations at the team level, as Data Teams use multiple sources of data to design yearly and quarterly goals. Tried-and-true suggestions for creating real-time, on-the-clock team conversations about using data photo albums for decisions provide principals and school leaders with realistic ways to begin. Chapter 3 is based on the imperative for principals and teachers to *stop losing their kids*. It includes recommendations for merging administrative, specialist, and classroom-teacher roles, and incorporates the conversations-based, double-instructed reading model for structured reading support. Sustainability, a culture of communication, and leadership capacity are discussed in Chapter 4.

Experts and practitioners in the field, including Jay McTighe, Douglas B. Reeves, Art Costa, Betsy Cunningham, and Barb Kapinus, share their wisdom and contribute their guiding voices throughout this book. It is my goal to integrate these authoritative voices into a framework that is immediately transferable to your particular setting. To that end, *Compelling Conversations* provides exhibits of the supportive leadership tools that are discussed throughout the book. These exhibits make the concepts described in the text immediately available to the reader. Interspersed throughout the book are authentic teacher, team, and student conversations exemplifying the following new concepts and outcomes related to a culture of conversations included in this book:

- Changing the slope of achievement one child at a time
- Predicting June achievement results in September
- Establishing individual student goals to achieve Invisible Excellence (more than one year's growth, even if students are still achieving below grade level) for students achieving below grade-level standards
- Assessing, measuring, and monitoring student performance with conversations throughout the year
- Interconnecting roles of leaders, teachers, and resource teachers to achieve shared accountability
- Establishing collaborative instructional models, including double-instructed reading, to increase standards of instruction

This book invites you to think differently about what assessment means, what roles are, and what instruction can look like. It is time to step beyond the museum's red-velvet barrier for a closer look at the portrait of learning. When you do, you'll notice that what you had been looking at has shifted, as teachers shift from saying, "All I want to do is teach," to "I want all my kids to learn."

As you read the following chapters, it is my hope that you, too, will feel compelled to write dates in your plan book for conversations with your teachers. Don't wait for the calendar to say "go," or for a day free from demands (that day will never come!). Instead, copy the letter to your teachers, fill in a date, and feel good that on this day you have committed to making a difference in all your students' lives.

Antique Cut Glass:
A Design for Conversations That Connect the Past to the Future

The "brilliant cut" design on my grandmother's cut glass begins with a small central point of two shapes connecting; it then spirals out in every direction, carving a complex, sparkling network deeply into the surface. Just like this design, Compelling Conversations spiral throughout a school learning community, carving new norms profoundly into the culture.

Compelling Conversations begin between the principal or school leader and the teacher, but these conversations then iterate throughout the school. Repeated interactions appear wherever teachers' interests about students interconnect, sealing their voices of concern deeply in their collaboration.

The Compelling Conversations pathway is not carved in stone; it is better represented in the richly intricate network of antique glass as the promise of a different reality. Shaped by beliefs and fueled by passions for every child's importance and achievement, let conversations become the voice, the calling, of your culture.

:: Thommie Piercy ::

Acknowledgments

My most humble appreciation goes to those incredible voices who have shaped mine: Art Costa's grand wisdom, shared during personal visits to my schools; Jay McTighe's intense intellect and insightful beliefs; Regie Routman's heart-rending letters about life; and Barb Kapinus's determined commitment to values. More recently, Douglas B. Reeves and his colleagues at The Leadership and Learning Center (formerly Center for Performance Assessment) have shown passionate vision and have demonstrated extraordinary devotion to student learning. These great leaders' significant difference is the depth of caring they personally demonstrate for individuals. I am grateful that my faith in conversations has remained in such good hands, resulting in the promise encompassed in this book.

I am fortunate to work with dedicated and inspiring teachers, including those of Mt. Airy Elementary School in Carroll County (Maryland). Their synergistic culture has resulted in remarkable hope for students' futures. My appreciation goes to the principals and teachers in and beyond the state whose conversations have enhanced outcomes for students. For the dedication of Sarah Curtis, Brooke Graves, and Anne Fenske and their rich gifts, including their editing talents, that resulted in an array of variables that contribute to student success being represented in this book, I am deeply grateful.

My most heartfelt gratitude goes to my husband, William. Daily, his positive spirit fills my heart with wisdom, love, and the true meaning of compassion beyond what I deserve. He is cherished for his insight that nourishes our growing family. It has been our son, Ian, whose spirit has stirred my thoughts through his writing and understanding since the days of his childhood. Ian possesses inner strength and courage beyond his years. His sensitivity provides inspiration and energy, especially in the kitchen at two in the morning! Our son Michael's heavenly soul continues to guide my direction, for which my heart is grateful. For Tracie and Jody's remarkable love of family, I am deeply thankful.

Lastly, I want to express my deep gratitude to my grandparents. How I wish we could continue our kitchen-table conversations so I could thank them for raising my dear sister, Teddy, and me on their farm. They filled our lives with values where the standard of the bell curve was established by determined beliefs, and the results were the pride of the harvest.

About the Author

THOMASINA DEPINTO PIERCY, Ph.D., earned her Ph.D. in Curriculum and Instruction with a focus on Reading and concentration in Human Resource Development from the University of Maryland in 1997. As a principal and a teacher, she spent 10 years teaching graduate reading and writing courses to educators from various states in the East Coast region. Dr. Piercy's research received the Reading Research Award from the State of Maryland International Reading Association. She was honored with the Bailor Award from McDaniel College for her distinguished career in education. As a teacher, she was named one of five expert teachers by the Maryland State Department of Education.

Dr. Piercy's previous publications include chapters in *Student Successes with Thinking Maps* (Corwin Press, forthcoming and 2004), *Learning and Leading with Habits of Mind* (ASCD, 2008), *Activating and Engaging Habits of Mind* (ASCD, 2000), *Integrating and Sustaining Habits of Mind* (ASCD, 2000), and *Step-Up-To-Excellence* (Scarecrow Press, 2002), a contribution to *Reading Essentials* (Heinemann, 2003), and articles in *Elementary School Journal*, and the *Journal for the Maryland Association of Supervision and Curriculum Development* (MASCD). In addition to being a professional development associate for The Leadership and Learning Center, Dr. Piercy is a trainer for Thinking Maps. She has presented at national conferences including the American Association of School Administrators (AASA), the Association for Supervision and Curriculum Development (ASCD), the International Reading Association (IRA), the National Staff Development Council (NSDC), and the International Conference on Thinking (ICOT).

As a former principal and current kindergarten through twelfth grade Supervisor of Reading for a school system in Maryland, Dr. Piercy has experience with every grade level. She has worked with The Leadership and Learning Center since 2006. She co-chairs the regional notMYkid organization, a parent resource for help and hope. She and her husband, William, share the pleasures of four children. They work in Maryland and live with their two dogs on the Shenandoah River, where they enjoy tubing, dancing, reading, and rich conversations! Dr. Piercy works in school districts interested in incorporating Compelling Conversations, Response to Intervention, and Data Team processes. She can be contacted at 304-725-3128, tpiercy@leadandlearn.com, or P.O. Box 1228, Harpers Ferry, WV 25425.

CHAPTER 1

CONVERSATIONS: *Increasing Student Achievement*

> **Essential Question:** *How can regularly scheduled conversations between school leaders and teachers increase student achievement?*

Chapter Foreword   ARTHUR L. COSTA

In the hectic, fast-paced, disjointed life of schools, we often fail to appreciate the power of structured, professional conversations. Although school personnel may engage in congenial teachers'-lounge chit-chat, precious little time is devoted to structured dialogue. And yet, through dialogue, we learn from processing our experiences and we enlarge our frame of reference beyond the episodic events of everyday school life. We know that holding conversations about work is essential to professional growth and development, because reflecting with others on experiences amplifies our insights and complex learnings.

Professional conversations are enriched when they are focused and structured; when all participants consciously use the tools of inquiry, data generation, and nonjudgmental behaviors; and when each member of a professional community takes an active role in the conversations, assumes a stance of exploration and experimentation, and exercises control over his or her own learning. As David

Perkins states, "Your organization functions and grows through conversations.... The quality of those conversations determines how smart your organization is" (2002).

An undeviating concentration on student learning is a core characteristic of professional communities. Teachers' professional actions focus on choices that affect students' opportunities to learn and provide substantial student benefit— and that is what this chapter is about. Through Compelling Conversations, teachers discuss the ways in which instruction promotes students' intellectual growth and development, as distinguished from simply focusing on activities or strategies that may engage students' attention.

Structured conversations are intentional. Holding truly Compelling Conversations requires one to follow a map (not a recipe). The intent is for a school leader (who may be an administrator or a colleague teacher) to engage teachers in thoughtful decision making about best practices for learners. The conversational "map" provides a framework in which data are surfaced, comparisons made, alternatives considered, outcomes predicted, consequences evaluated, and learnings summarized.

Conversations that engage reflective practice imply self-awareness about one's work as a teacher. By engaging in in-depth conversations about teaching and learning, teachers can examine the assumptions basic to quality practice. Compelling Conversations concern the school and instructional problems of learning, as well as questions of student development and progress. Conversations that invite reflection on practice lead to deepened understanding of the process of instruction and of the products created through the teaching and learning process.

Professional educational communities wishing to improve their practices and student achievement will find this chapter enlightening and challenging. However, school staffs should be prepared to demand ongoing inquiry, effect substantial changes in practice, challenge existing norms of privacy and autonomy, and question existing practices and assumptions about students. Be assured as you do that the benefits far outweigh the challenges. Not only will students profit, but there will also be an increase in the collaborative focus on student learning and effective teaching, a building of greater trust and professionalism, and the sharing of a common vision among the staff.

Introduction

Compelling Conversations drive out fear of test scores and replace that fear with focused confidence in student learning. These regularly scheduled conversations between the administrative team and each teacher yield immediate data, which become a centerpiece of shared accountability with Data Teams (The Leadereship and Learning Ceneter, formerly Center for Performance Assessment, 2006) for student progress *during* the year. Particularly because of its inclusion of backward-mapping of students' goals (McTighe & Wiggins, 2004) and frequent monitoring of their progress (with teachers), the Compelling Conversations process is unprecedented in cutting through barriers of norms hidden within traditional, isolated decisions. Student success, as evidenced in the triangulated hard-data results, make these conversations compelling.

As a future-oriented student achievement process, Compelling Conversations with teachers push traditional student achievement limits by focusing on *teacher-generated*, formative student data in the form of student goals. Teachers include this data, along with student work, so that their Data Teams can write monthly student achievement goals (Schmoker, 2001). These Data Team goals are monitored and revisited on an ongoing basis to link instruction and achievement. Therefore, conversations at the Data Team level are supported and monitored through conversations between the administrative team and individual practitioners. This layered approach, which allows a view of student achievement through multiple lenses, ensures that teachers have the resources they need to help students achieve learning goals.

Several key features distinguish Compelling Conversations from other processes:

- Data having *predictive* qualities and value are generated during Compelling Conversations. The formative data are backward-mapped from June to forecast student achievement outcomes on state assessments.

- The slope of achievement is changed one child at a time, one grade at a time, and one school over time.

- Frequent, collaborative monitoring of *every* student's achievement is completed with each teacher.

- Bell-curve expectations are discarded in favor of established, measurable goals for each and every child, leading to accountability that is student-centered (Reeves, 2004).

- Data generated from these conversations (Piercy, 2003) become internal data for each teacher and Data Teams.

- Data Teams regularly establish goals (Schmoker, 2001) using outcomes from Compelling Conversations.

- Adult behaviors in need of attention (Reeves, 2005), such as embracing accountability for student achievement and making data-based instructional decisions, are transformed through direct and individualized guidance during Compelling Conversations.

■ The principal and leadership team acquire immediate, insightful, and specific indicators directly from teachers regarding "next-action thinking" (Sparks, 2005, p. 157) for school improvement.

■ Understanding the story behind the numbers links assessment to instruction (Reeves, 2004).

These compelling aspects of conversations lead to the development of a culture of accountability that is embraced rather than feared. Data generated during Compelling Conversations support a culture of shared knowledge and decision making (DuFour, DuFour, Eaker, & Karhanek, 2004). This results in student learning that is transferable, as evidenced by the relationship between the data outcomes of conversations and the significant, sustained results on high-stakes assessments. For example, in the third year, 96 percent of Maryland's Mt. Airy Elementary exiting students (entering middle school) were reading proficiently, as shown by internal 2004–2005 Compelling Conversation data. These results aligned with the high-stakes Maryland School Assessment summative data, which reported that 98.6 percent of exiting students were reading proficiently.

In addition to remarkable gains in student achievement, Compelling Conversations nurture growth toward a positive culture of accountability. Accountability shared among teachers, teams, and administrators establishes a culture of respect, trust, excellence, and enthusiastic commitment to teamwork as the source of success for students. As these scheduled conversations iterate through excited teams, faculty rooms, copier lines, and the hallways, sustaining change *between* grade levels, teachers are saying, "I like using this data. Each year I can determine expectations for my students more clearly. Then, I know what I need to teach." New teacher/administrative team communication patterns develop into accountability that is no longer avoided or feared, but welcomed as teachers hold students' success in their hands.

The question most frequently asked about Compelling Conversations has been: "The concept of talking with individual teachers about each student is so logical and powerful; why haven't we always done this?" When the administrative team and each teacher meet about every student's progress, they establish a connection between high standards and learning. This book offers a clear framework for conducting Compelling Conversations that combines reflective practice about student progress, data, and assessment to improve student achievement for each child, each class, each grade, and ultimately each school. The remarkable effectiveness of these conversations stems from the fact that they bring the real and perceived barriers of student achievement and the invisible norms of practice to the surface, where they can be recognized, analyzed, and dealt with.

Losing Our Kids: The Origins of Compelling Conversations

I had no idea why our superintendent wanted to talk to me!

His brief remarks had lasting meaning: I was being appointed the principal of our district's most overcrowded school, which was housed in a nearly 70-year-old building and whose students had floundering test scores. Nevertheless, I was excited.

During my initial walk-through, a question kept occurring to me, as though shouted from the (leaky) rooftop: *Why are students, including those with no identified learning problems or IEPs, performing below their enrolled grade level?* The large number of students being provided reading instruction one to two years below their expected level grabbed my heart and mind. Yes, our swelling population, increasing to more than 800 students, was requiring a playground full of trailers. With six to eight teachers per grade, more than one-fourth of the staff nontenured, and structural water leakage problems, my attention could easily have been diverted from the critical concern: only 39 percent of our grade 3, non-Title I students were achieving the state goal of "satisfactory" on the Maryland high-stakes state reading assessment—and the acceptable score for the "satisfactory" state standard was only 70 percent!

Discovering the Root Cause

Working backward from the desired result (McTighe & Wiggins, 2004) that all students perform on or above their enrolled grade level, our first goal was to understand the root cause of decisions that resulted in students not making a year's progress for each year in school. I began with our fourth- and fifth-grade teachers, asking, "Why are you providing reading instruction two years below students' enrolled grade level?"

The response? "That was the level students were reading on when they entered school this year."

Such responses were brutally honest and consistent, the symptom clear: *We were losing our kids.* The problem was evident: *No one understood why.*

Troubling Truth

In teachers' responses, I heard my own voice. Years of teaching kindergarten through fifth-grade students helped me recognize and acknowledge the troubling truth. Teachers' responses were harshly honest, and revealed a systemic tendency toward reliance on independent, fragmented decisions as the driving influences on student progress. As Michael Fullen, a guiding force in concepts related to leadership, explains, "The central tendency of dynamic, complex systems is to constantly generate, overload, and cause fragmentation" (2001, p. 108).

Dedicated and caring teachers simply did not know *how* students arrived with no IEPs at the beginning of the school year already one or more years behind. During my 18 years as a teacher, I had always thought *somebody* knew how my students were progressing after they moved on to the next grade. As a principal, I looked around in vain for that person: you know, the one who would know how all the children were doing from one year to the next. Who *should* know? The reading teacher? The counselor? As the realization intruded into my awareness that it was vital for all of us to begin to know and understand the progress of each student in the school, I took a very long, deep breath.

I began asking, "We're losing our kids! What can we *do*?"

While talking with and listening to teachers, the problem became clear, as I heard the most common reply again and again: "I don't really *know*. Whatever decisions were made in previous grades that resulted in my students, including those with no IEPs, being one year or more behind, I do not understand."

The unwelcome truth had finally been revealed. The root cause of decisions that resulted in students not reading on or above their enrolled grade level remained invisible, behind doors inadvertently locked by years of traditionally accepted practice. Every culture is a reflection of "hidden history" (Barth, 2002). In education, this hidden history influences decisions throughout a school: the culture, which has been built up over time, can be either a facilitator of change or a barrier to change.

At times, when I need to see things differently, I turn to literature for ideas. The words of Lewis Carroll (1865, p. 15) influenced my next steps: "There were doors all round the hall, but they were locked." The "doors" of teacher decisions had been closed and locked by years of established traditions. This is the opposite of the desired norm, "professionals regularly collaborating in an effort to define and reach goals" (Schmoker, 1999, p. 11).

After becoming aware of the symptom, recognizing the problem was the first step. Acknowledging openly that *we did not understand why students fall behind* removed the invisibility of the problem, and made it obvious that we needed to find out more about what decisions result in students' falling behind. Lack of communication was the root cause, and communication was the path that would lead to resolving the problem.

⇢ ***Symptom:*** Students, including those with no identified learning problems, were reading one to two years below their enrolled grade levels.

⇢ ***Problem:*** No one, including the administrators, understood why!

⇢ ***Root Cause:*** Lack of communication.

In conjunction with the challenging expectations created by the No Child Left Behind act (NCLB), the powerful honesty in teachers' statements surfaced the true state of affairs: teachers do not really understand why students having no IEPs are coming to them performing below grade-level standards. As Schmoker explained, "We must take advantage of data's capacity to prompt collaborative dialogue" (1999, p. 46). Teachers' comments clearly validated the urgency of improving communication about student achievement through focused, data-based conversations.

The Need for Compelling Conversations

Although all learning involves conversations, "there are too few conversations in too few places—no active listening or compromising, no exchanges, no discussion of curriculum, no taking seriously the feedback from teachers." Regie Routman's heart-rending statement (2000, p. xxxvi) provided the premise for significant conversations. The student achievement results generated by Compelling Conversations indicated that we had not previously relied on our greatest natural resources, our teachers.

No analysis of external standardized scores can provide more or better information as to areas where change is needed than the voices of teachers. However, teacher recommendations have traditionally been made at the end of the school year, and that's it. Teachers' common message pinpointed the problem: no one clearly understood exactly why each student arrived at the beginning of the year, or had progressed from kindergarten through grade 5, designated to work on a particular level of instruction. How could they? Cumulative folders with report-card documentation are stored in locked office files. Confidential special education files are locked in a different room. The increase in the number of retiring teachers is matched only by the increase in the number of transient families. All these factors combine to prevent teachers from acquiring the full story about a child from year to year.

Conversations are based on assessments while taking into account the expertise of teachers, what teachers stand for, and what teachers are about.

Teachers have not had sufficient knowledge of or understanding about decisions made at previous grade levels concerning children. Without this knowledge, how could we be certain that each student was working up to his or her potential? Within this problem accountability resided.

Arousing student-centered accountability (Reeves, 2004) from its dormant state requires a most fundamental, yet powerful, shift in thinking. No longer can we opt for the triage approach to school improvement. For example, we could have set a priority that students having no learning disabilities must receive instruction *on* their grade level. However, attacking a *symptom* in isolation, such as students not performing up to their capabilities, does not resolve a *problem*. Without a change in thinking—not a new layer of work or mandates, but a real change in the roles of the administrative team and supporting Data Teams—students' progress *during* the school year, and into the next grade, will continue to fall into a black hole of unused and basically useless data.

Conversations: A Validated Form of Assessment

Art Costa (1991) explains *humility* as knowing that we do not know—and admitting it. Even in the role of principal, I did not understand why we were losing our kids, and admitting that took both humility and courage. That admission, however, helps to dissolve dependence on school improvement assessment systems and assessment data that are neither sufficiently complete nor timely enough to be helpful. When leaders do not know *where* their students are as learners *during* the school year, do not *know* that we are losing kids, and do not *understand why* we are losing them, they cannot lead effectively. We need different information.

As depicted in Exhibit 1.1, data generated during Compelling Conversations have formative assessment qualities that inform teachers and Data Teams. Because they are ongoing and provide specific feedback about students' current achievement performance, data from conversations with individual teachers upend the concept of top-down, whole-school data by providing information that communicates all students' needs in real time. In this way, the administrative team can consider the intense, end-of-year state assessment outcomes, but act on them immediately through focused, frequent, consistent monitoring of students' assessment based on progress *during* the school year. Marzano's research synthesis (2003) states that of the five school-level factors that affect student achievement, effective feedback and goals with frequent monitoring are second only to having a guaranteed and viable curriculum. Frequent monitoring of feedback and goals is the foundation of accountability that is student-centered.

◎◎
EXHIBIT 1.1 **Formative Assessment Qualities of Compelling Conversations Data**

ESSENTIAL QUESTION: How can we measure learning?

School Improvement with Summative Data	School Improvement with Formative Compelling Conversations Data
▪ Think big, start big; top-down data	▪ Think big, start small; bottom-up data
▪ Autopsy report: school is over, too late, kids not coming back to that grade	▪ Individual, student-centered accountability
▪ Burnt-cookies syndrome: next batch will be better—but what about this batch?	▪ Invisible excellence discovered
▪ School improvement plan is completed for central office; due date for plan may be prior to the release of previous assessment outcomes	▪ Beliefs drive action
	▪ Data help articulate monthly Data Team goals
	▪ Individual students are named and discussed
▪ School goals for current year cannot be informed	▪ Frequent, consistent monitoring of data
▪ Accountability is *done to* teachers	▪ Midpoint, ongoing corrections
	▪ Deterioration and abandonment of bell curve
	▪ Slope of school achievement is changed one child at a time
	▪ Just-in-time professional development
	▪ Articulation of best practices
	▪ Culture of shared, data-based decision making
	▪ Invisible norms dispelled
	▪ Trust in colleagues built and enhanced
	▪ Increased teacher leadership capacity
	▪ Assessment measures crafted by teachers
	▪ Shared accountability is owned

The bottom line is that a child's learning is not directly improved as a result of autopsy reports in the form of high-stakes assessment printouts downloaded from state and district Web sites. Douglas Reeves (2002, p. 51) describes high achievement results that occur under conditions where the causes are not clearly understood as "Lucky." In contrast, high results accompanied by understanding of the predictors of achievement are described as "Leading," because there is a greater likelihood of replication. Conversations between individual teachers and the administrative team provide opportunities to collaboratively modify instructional decisions and later improve every teacher's capacity to understand the causes of student performance by collaboratively reflecting on the results of the decisions. The potential for replication of successful decisions is increased through regular, focused conversations about each student's progress. As teachers and administrative teams track students' successes, those practices that improved performance—the "antecedents of excellence"—will be pinpointed, refined, and shared throughout the school or district (White, 2005). Therefore, what data we use and how we use data directly affect our ability to improve the trajectory of learning for students and for an organization.

Changing the Slope of Student Achievement

Genuine snapshots of learning are not taken by state assessments. End-of-year data cannot change that year's outcomes. State assessment data outcomes are frequently represented visually as a line graph that has an increased slope, denoting the state-required increase in scores. Individual school outcomes are plotted on and compared to the state-required projections. However, knowing the slope of a school's achievement cannot change the slope of a *student's* achievement. Collecting data does not change the slope of learning. Focusing on the need to change the overall learning slope of a school diverts attention from where the change must occur: the slope of the individual child. By the *slope* of a child's achievement, I am referring to the increase in that student's growth and knowledge during the school year, as measured by informal and formal assessments.

Why is the slope of individual achievement important? If a child is reading one year below his or her enrolled grade level, that student's performance typically remains on that trajectory or path throughout his or her entire school career. These students usually are the ones pulled out of their grade-level instruction for remediation, which results in them falling even further behind grade-level standards. A decision made by one teacher can result in such a child never having the opportunity to achieve grade-level standards. However, if we change the slope— that is, the curve of learning—to achieve two years' growth in one year's time, then we have changed the slope of that student's learning trajectory. We need to help teachers understand how to move the distribution of students upward to the next decile (Bernhardt, 2002) and to the right.

As a principal, I am committed to stopping our loss of kids. At a conference on NCLB, Joe Torgesen (2004) explained that the growth trajectory for below-grade-level students will not result in them reading on their enrolled grade level. They need something strong enough to place them on a growth trajectory with a sustained trend demonstrating an increased number of students performing on grade-level standards. It is time to shelve the bell curve by not accepting its inherent premise that it is okay to lose some students.

Constructing a Different Reality of Assessment

The cardinal principle of measurement is: "It is more important and accurate to measure a few things frequently and consistently, than to measure many things once" (Reeves, 2004, p. 25); this principle is the basis for Compelling Conversations. How frequently you schedule these conversations will depend on the processes that are currently in place and each school's desired outcomes. Meeting with individual teachers monthly or quarterly to consider each student's progress provides targeted scaffolding for each teacher's instructional decisions about every student's achievement. The data results of the conversations inform the Data Team (which meets once or more each month) so that its members can set, review, and revise team goals based on students' strengths and obstacles. Some schools schedule Compelling Conversations in six-week cycles or quarterly. Marzano's research indicates that "at a minimum, students should receive quarterly feedback on their academic performance" (2003, p. 39).

Initially, I scheduled conversations monthly. Gradually, as teachers began initiating conversations independently with one another, across grade levels and with specialists, and as our Data Teams became more experienced, the Compelling Conversations between individual teachers and our administrative team began to be scheduled quarterly. Schools' scheduling will vary depending on students' needs and the current structures in place to monitor students. *Compelling Conversations do not replace Data Teams, administrative teams, or student support teams; rather, they augment that work by increasing coherence around standards established by school-based teamwork.*

During these regularly scheduled conversations, participants focus on formative assessments of every student's current performance and expected progress, not summative test scores alone. Marzano's research (2003, p. 39) strongly recommends reducing reliance "on results from standardized state tests as the primary feedback mechanism to assess students' learning." Instead, use results from formative assessments, which include both formal and informal methods, such as ungraded quizzes, oral questioning, and teacher observations (McTighe & O'Conner, 2005). The capacity of the Compelling Conversations process to generate formative data frequently for each teacher's class and about every student results in the data being a superb resource for Data Teams.

In conversations about each student, the real story of accountability is told through the voice of teachers and the accurate eyes of their measurable student goals. "Either we are reduced to test scores or we seize the opportunity to tell the real story of educational accountability" (Reeves, 2004, p. 25). Characteristics of accountability that are evident in Compelling Conversations include:

- Having an individual student-centered focus
- Providing timely results leading to immediate interventions
- Acquiring data results that reliably predict outcomes of external state assessments
- Building trust among teachers
- Focusing on increased achievement for every grade (not only state-selected grades) and for each student, including special education students

What is the real story behind the numbers? As the results of Compelling Conversations with individual teachers are transformed into teacher-generated data, and as these individual student data are included in the Data Team's goal setting (see Chapter 2), data become transparent at a deep, ethical level: we know and understand when and why we *begin* losing our kids. This is assessment information that is useful and timely; curriculum modifications proceed as soon as the need is indicated. *It is during Compelling Conversations between the teacher and the administrative team that the slope of a child's achievement can be changed.* One child at a time, one teacher at a time, one grade at a time, and one school *over* time, the slope of achievement increases (see Exhibit 1.2).

Each time one more child achieves success on grade-level standards, class standards are improved. As a class improves, the grade-level performance

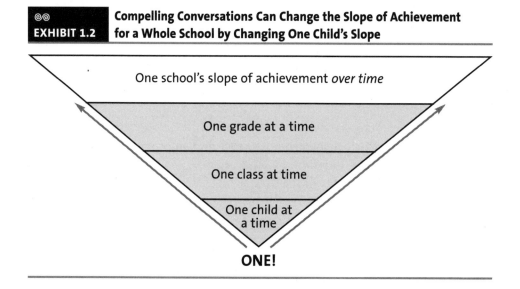

◎◎
EXHIBIT 1.2 **Compelling Conversations Can Change the Slope of Achievement for a Whole School by Changing One Child's Slope**

One school's slope of achievement *over time*

One grade at a time

One class at time

One child at a time

ONE!

increases. When each grade advances in proficiency, the whole school improves. The slope of a school is changed one child at time. Improvement begins with one: for example, the U-2 singer, Bono, shared the title of "2005 Man of the Year" for his personal efforts to alleviate world poverty and AIDS in South Africa. Stephen Covey agrees; he explains that most culture shifts "start ... with the choice of one person, regardless of position. Such moral authority inspires and lifts others" (2004, p. 25). I'm not talking about a revolution—just one conversation with one teacher, talking about one child.

All students deserve this attention. Isn't that right? Not just our special education students or struggling readers. *All students deserve our time,* our conversation about their learning. Becky Brill, principal of a middle school in Hardy County West Virginia that had experienced reconstitution pursuant to No Child Left Behind legislation and is now successful, explained after completing Compelling Conversations with her teachers, "I love this. These conversations force me to sit down and know all these students also." Becky stated that she believed she knew her students before having conversations, but now she understands them better. Regie Routman (2003, p. 5) explains, "One of the best ways I know to be knowledgeable is to engage in ongoing professional conversations. Without ongoing professional conversations in our schools, we are at the mercy of politicians and publishers who think they should determine how and what we should be teaching." Student-centered accountability is not "done to" teachers, because teachers "actively participate in the development, refinement and reporting of accountability" (Reeves, 2004, p. 3).

Accountability reaches its potential as a welcomed and constructive force because it is not just about summative test scores that "summarize what students have learned at the conclusion of an instructional segment" (McTighe & O'Conner, 2005, p. 11). Accountability lives in the hearts of teachers who *care about kids.* This is what teachers do best!

"In the present controversies over accountability, the prevailing allegation is that test scores are 'hard data' whereas teaching practices are 'soft' and, by implication, less worthy. Such a dichotomy is unproductive and false" (Reeves, 2004, p. 25). It is imperative that indicators of adult behaviors, such as teaching practices, be included in accountability systems (Reeves, 2005). Such behaviors are shaped and guided during Compelling Conversations. Our Compelling Conversations humanize accountability by talking about joys and disappointments for both students and teachers. Problems are shared by the principal, assistant principal, school leaders, and the entire team, because we are all on the same mission.

As explained by Stephen White, an author and leader in accountability regarding data analysis, "Accountability is taking action on the basis of what the data tells us and acting quickly on the diagnosis, rather than allowing problems to fester"

(2005, p. 79). Conversations frequently include how to raise standards for students performing both above and below their enrolled grade levels. This holistic accountability (Reeves, 2004) includes not only specific information about teaching practices (the decisions made by adults), but also opportunities to shape specific decisions with every teacher. The significance of Compelling Conversations' ability to expand teacher capacity is reflected in Schmoker's statement that "research in business and education demonstrates that leadership is essential to substantive and enduring progress" (1999, p. 72). Yet, the literature reveals a lack of strategic leadership that focuses on improving instruction. Studies by Smith and Andrews (1989) show that "a principal's day seldom reflects any meaningful influence on what goes on in the classroom" (Schmoker, 2001, p. 72). Therefore, Compelling Conversations bring administration and teachers to the instructional discussion through systematic and systemic data analysis.

Compelling Conversations Influence Student Achievement

The power of Compelling Conversations is reflected in the experience of a U.S. Army photojournalist. During a layover at the airport, en route to speak at the ASCD convention, a uniformed soldier shared my crowded bench. I inquired about his assignment. He explained that he was returning to Iraq by choice. He surprised me by saying that he had the greatest job in the world and had requested to return. As our conversation continued, I learned that this soldier was a combat photographer for the United States Army. In describing his responsibilities as a photojournalist, his voice became passionate as he revealed that while facing one of his greatest challenges, he had captured a photo of a battle that encompassed the soul of the war. His remarkable picture ended up on the desk of the Commander of Allied Forces in Iraq. The photo was sent with a report on the fighting to the Department of Defense. Later, during a visit to Iraq, the Secretary of Defense looked up this soldier and explained to him that the picture he had taken had influenced the decision about remaining in Iraq.

This soldier said he was returning to Iraq because he realized that "*a picture can change a war!*" It's true: a single picture can profoundly affect future decisions.

As a school principal, I am no soldier. Photojournalists are not becoming embedded in education, but saving a child from getting lost in isolated decisions is worth going to battle. Just as a soldier's picture changed a war, images of students' outcomes can change the direction of educational decisions. Visual representations of student achievement can make a dramatic difference in the outcome of additional students' lives if conversations become one of the initial and prevailing forces for decisions within schools.

Compelling Conversations Results Correlate with District and State Data

How compelling are these conversations about student achievement? The results predicted by our conversations were confirmed by school, district, and state data, establishing a three-point triangulation of data. The term *triangulation* is used to "determine needs or targets from diverse types of data" (White, 2005, p. 108). White explains that triangulation leads to the question: "What can we glean from the interaction of these factors?" (2005, p. 108). Such questions provide the foundation for data-driven decision making (The Leadership and Learning Center, formerly Center for Performance Assessment, 2004). As you will note, our exiting students achieved more than 90 percent proficiency in reading; our special education subgroup also achieved more than 90 percent. During our quarterly Compelling Conversations, teachers predicted these state assessment outcomes. The predictive relationship between conversations and high-stakes state assessments must be kept in perspective: although each student's performance has come a long way, the significant aspect is that teachers *do* know their students as learners. Knowing students this accurately means that throughout the year, teachers can make midcourse corrections to guide students effectively in reaching their potential.

Exhibit 1.3 represents the close correlation, or triangulation, of internal Compelling Conversations results and external data results for the school year

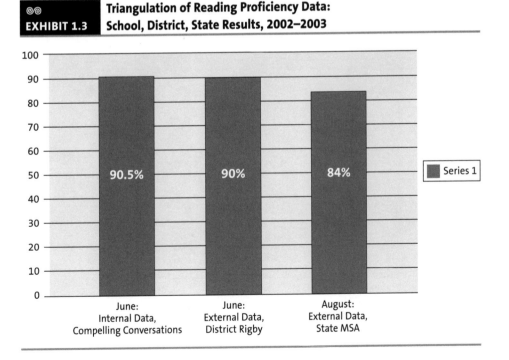

EXHIBIT 1.3 **Triangulation of Reading Proficiency Data: School, District, State Results, 2002–2003**

June: Internal Data, Compelling Conversations — 90.5%
June: External Data, District Rigby — 90%
August: External Data, State MSA — 84%

Series 1

2002–2003. Posted the first week of June, the results state that 90.5 percent of students are receiving reading instruction on or above grade level. The external district data (received after the teachers and students went on summer vacation) show that 90 percent of our students are reading on or above grade level. The Maryland high-stakes data, reported in August, showed that 84 percent of our students were reading on or above grade-level standards. These data reveal that teachers accurately projected, within 6.5 percent, the results of student performance on the 2002–2003 Maryland assessments.

Exhibit 1.4 depicts scores from the following year, 2003–2004, that correlate with and form a triangulation among Compelling Conversations stages (which are a form of assessment of student progress), the district-level Rigby reading assessments, and the state-level Maryland school assessment (MSA). Teachers' projections about the high-stakes assessments were nearly 98 percent accurate.

Significantly, this correlation indicates that:

1. There is a predictive connection between Compelling Conversations data and high-stakes assessment outcomes.

2. Compelling Conversations are a form of assessment of student achievement that is accurate and effective in informing teachers' instructional decisions.

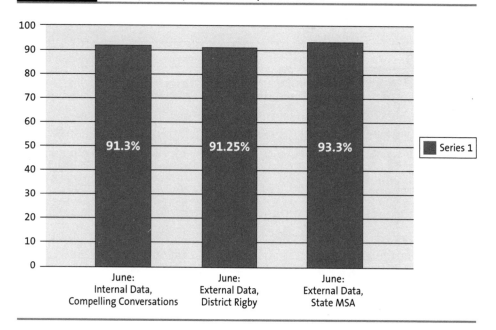

◉◉
EXHIBIT 1.4   **Triangulation of Reading Proficiency Data: School, District, State Results, 2003–2004**

- June: Internal Data, Compelling Conversations — 91.3%
- June: External Data, District Rigby — 91.25%
- June: External Data, State MSA — 93.3%

3. The standards for performance within the classroom are increased through backward mapping of goals.

The correlation also highlights what we have already discovered: that the experts—our teachers—are among us. Therefore, it is crucial that we make time in our schedules to have conversations with our teachers, so that they can increase their knowledge of and understanding about the needs of their students. This is supported by Marzano's statement: "All researchers agree that the impact of decisions made by individual teachers is far greater than the impact of decisions made at the school level" (2003, p. 71). In fact, Marzano concluded that research "dramatically illustrates the profound impact an individual teacher can have on student achievement" (p. 72).

Expensive, prepackaged programs for low-performing students are not needed when teachers' expertise is respected and their capacity to accurately forecast the needs of their learners is tapped in September. The regular monitoring done through Compelling Conversations and the collaborative decisions made by teachers and the administrative team, establish high standards. The predictions are borne out by the end-of-year Compelling Conversation data indicating that 91.3 percent of students would be performing on and above the grade-level standard determined by the district. This Compelling Conversation projection was 98 percent accurate for the 2003–2004 Maryland state assessment outcomes of 93.3 percent.

Results Replicated and Predicted

Replicated again in 2004–2005, Compelling Conversation data projected that 96 percent of our exiting students would be reading proficiently. District Rigby assessments indicated that 92 percent of our students were in fact reading proficiently at grade level. Later, when the state high-stakes assessment outcomes were posted, 98.6 percent of our students were found to be reading proficiently (see Exhibit 1.5). Notice that the 2.6 percent discrepancy in our teachers' predictions was on the low side of the actual state outcome!

The predictive quality of Compelling Conversations is represented as well in Exhibit 1.6, where the end-of-year average of Compelling Conversations data documented teachers' statements in assessed grades that 92 percent of their students were achieving grade-level or above reading standards. These data were distributed to teachers at the end of the year and posted in the front hall. During summer vacation, the district reading assessment, the Rigby, reported that 92 percent of the students were reading on or above grade level. The Maryland school assessments confirmed the average for assessed grades: 91.7 percent of students were reading on

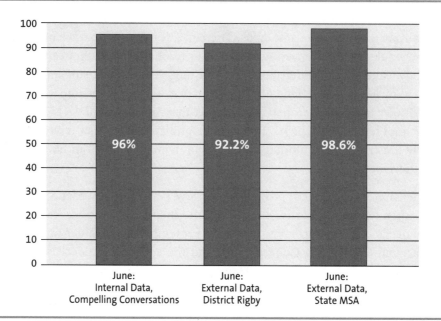

EXHIBIT 1.5 — Triangulation of Reading Proficiency Data: School, District, State Results, 2004–2005

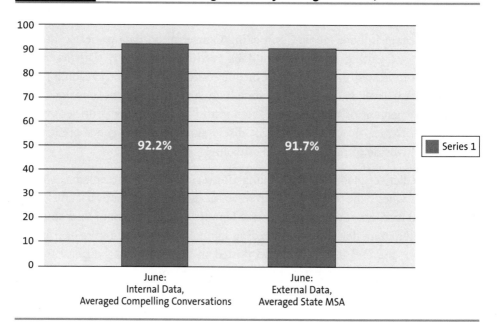

EXHIBIT 1.6 — Predictive Quality of Averaged Compelling Conversations re State MSA Reading Proficiency Averaged Results, 2004–2005

or above grade level. When teachers understand their students this well to start with, we can provide targeted support throughout the school year, beginning with our first September conversations, to help all students achieve success.

Subgroups Excel

The gender gap was a very tough data point for us to budge. However, as our conversations focused on suggestions for increasing expectations of our boys, the gap of 32 percent of males underperforming females closed completely, to 0 percent. By rejecting the bell-curve philosophy that some students will inevitably be low performers (such as boys being low-performing in reading), and replacing that with an expectation that all students will achieve proficiency, we gradually closed the gender gap.

Exhibit 1.7 shows that in the special education subgroup, 84.2 percent of students performed proficiently. This is within 1.5 percent of the district's proficiency score expected of *all* students. Compare this with the district average score for special education students of 41.9 percent. Such an accomplishment for these students reflects a deep shift in beliefs. A robust belief system, as is present in Data Teams and individual teachers, supports and enables these results.

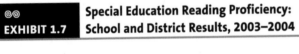

Special Education Reading Proficiency:
School and District Results, 2003–2004

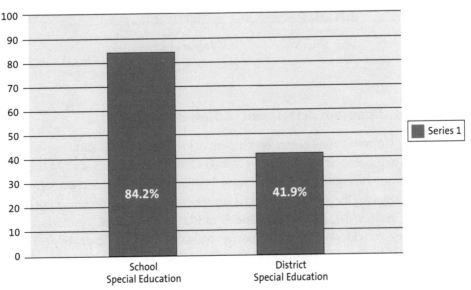

In 2005, the exiting special education students performed at 95.3 percent (see Exhibit 1.8). This compared to our overall exiting student scores of 98.6 percent. The special education students' scores were 36.1 percent higher than the district scores, and higher than the average district scores for the *proficient* students! Our student enrollment consists of the district's average number of identified special education students and county average for gifted and talented students. Neither subgroup is spiked in a particular direction.

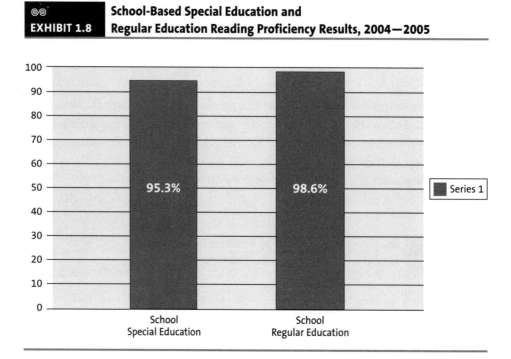

EXHIBIT 1.8   **School-Based Special Education and Regular Education Reading Proficiency Results, 2004—2005**

Achievement through Assessment: A Summary

Compelling Conversations center on student achievement goals and ways to help all students achieve their potential. High-stakes assessment scores are not the goal or focus of our dialogue. Superior results are the *effect* of instruction based on conversations (see Chapter 3) that focus on frequent monitoring and midcourse corrections in a few areas, as recommended in Black and Wiliam's research (1998), which states conclusively that formative assessment does improve learning. Additionally, having a balanced success to effort ratio motivates everyone (McTighe, 2006).

Compelling Conversations results are dramatic. The commitment is deep. The process is simple: one commitment, abundant results.

Six Basic Questions about Getting Started with Compelling Conversations

Where do I find time for Compelling Conversations? Stephen Covey (1994) reminds us that to find time for the important activities, we must not prioritize the schedule, but schedule our priorities. Finding time for Compelling Conversations is a big "rock" that can fit in your agenda if you put it in first. Then, all the other demands will fit in around it. Get your schedule and check for yourself to see if there is just one free day in the next nine weeks. If so, you have time to begin!

1. How much *time* will I spend with each teacher?

When I began scheduling time for conversations with all classroom teachers, we met every month. Eventually, as teamwork structures and additional conversations increased, we found we could reduce the frequency of scheduled conversations. This will vary by school, depending on the specificity of the school's teamwork structures and the needs of its students. Scheduling one day in September to discuss initial student information establishes the foundation for monitoring student data. For transient populations, entrance and exit conferences provide students with every opportunity to achieve their best while they are with you. Frequently, this data can be forwarded to another school in the area. Therefore, beginning in September, and then each month or marking period, one day for Compelling Conversations is scheduled directly on the school calendar hanging in the office and e-mailed through our weekly newsletter. The teachers and administrative team appreciate having time designated to meet and focus on each child's progress because it increases accuracy of communication, including that to the homes of our students. Also, it ensures that time is scheduled into the school day to monitor all students' goals and achievement of the next instructional benchmarks. Face-to-face conversations with each teacher about all students—and each student—is a most cost-effective use of time. Also, the immediate, predictive data as to high-stakes assessment outcomes are used by Data Teams (see Chapter 2).

2. How can I *get started*?

Just schedule Compelling Conversations for one day each month or marking period, plus one day in September. If you missed September, go ahead and get started now. One principal began after attending a national conference on

Compelling Conversations in April; she said she did not want to wait until September!

Copy the letter in Exhibit 1.9 to send to your teachers. Then, buy some chocolates to have available during the sessions, and you are on your way to excellent conversations!

EXHIBIT 1.9	**Letter to Teacher from Principal/Leadership Team Member: Beginning Compelling Conversations**

Date: _____

Good Morning!
A day has been planned for us to have conversations about your students.
My desired outcome is to have more time for us to talk individually about your students so that we can collaborate about their goals. Also, I want to provide any additional resources that I have to support you and your students in achieving goals for this year.

Our day for the school-wide Compelling Conversations will be _____.

I will have a "floater" substitute for the day so that we can spend about 20 minutes together. You will <u>not</u> need to write plans for the sub. Some suggestions for the substitute are:

- Provide student newspapers for them to use, such as *Time for Kids*
- Provide independent reading time for students
- Continue with the same lesson
- Provide time for a writing workshop

Our conversation will <u>not</u> interrupt your planning time or lunch period!

Please put a copy of the performance levels on which you are providing instruction for each of your students in my mailbox by _____.
Just bring your most recent data about your students; this data can be in the form of assessments, your grade book, and/or student work that will enrich our conversation.

I am really looking forward to our conversation.

Sincerely,

If you schedule three days for conferences the first year (September, January, and June), you will garner initial, midyear, and end-of-year data. Though the meetings are not frequent, this timing permits teachers, administrative teams, and Data Teams to begin working regularly with powerful, predictive-quality data generated by individual teachers for every student.

3. What might a *schedule* for Compelling Conversations look like?

Scheduling time to meet with teachers during the work day sends the clear message that their time is valued. Hiring one substitute teacher for one to one-and-one-half days each marking period provides enough time to meet with every classroom teacher individually. This collaboration is a building block for establishing professional learning communities (Eaker, DuFour, & DuFour, 2002), because the teachers and administrators contribute as partners toward student progress.

The schedule shown in Exhibit 1.10 lists teachers' names, but no time frame (the time for conversations should be flexible). This will be the teachers' release time for conversations. Whenever possible, we hired the same person as our substitute for all five days during the school year because familiarity with the school building made the sub more time efficient. Just copy the same schedule for the remaining Compelling Conversations later in the year!

The following details help to make the day of Compelling Conversations go smoothly:

- List all classroom teachers on the schedule
- Plan for a minimum of 20 minutes per conversation
- Explain that the schedule is designed to allow the substitute teacher to cycle into classrooms
- Point out that the schedule is flexible because some conversations will require more time
- Do not interrupt any teacher during lunch or planning time for conversations
- Have the substitute go to the next person until lunch is over
- Schedule 30 minutes for lunch for the substitute and the administrative team
- Provide the substitute with a copy of the schedule

Teachers plan differently for the time during which they are out of the classroom. Their decisions will vary according to the subject they are teaching at the time. The main goal is to keep the activity simple, to avoid having teachers spend

◉◉
EXHIBIT 1.10 **Schedule for the Floating Substitute**

This schedule is the order in which our substitute will come to your classrooms. Please bring a group list of your students, the level at which you are currently delivering instruction for each student, and any recent assessments.

Compelling Conversations Substitute Schedule   **Date:** _____

ORDER (approx. 20 min. per teacher)

Teacher Name

1.
2.
3.
4.
5.
6.
7.
8.
9.
10.
11.
12.
13.
14.
15.
16.
17.
18.
19.
20.
21.
22.
23.
24.
25.

their planning time writing plans for the short time they will be away from the classroom. Some examples of activities for the substitute include:

■ Continue the teacher's same lesson

■ Provide students with independent reading time to read their library books

■ Have a student newspaper available, such as *Time for Kids*

■ Let students read or write independently

4. With my budget, can I *afford* to schedule Compelling Conversations?

The cost of a substitute each month or marking period is the total expense for incorporating Compelling Conversations. Even during a time of budget reductions, the expense of just one substitute is manageable. Consider this: No student's limitations will go unnoticed, because every child will be expected to make one year's growth or more, and the administrative team will contribute to every child's progress. What priority could be more deserving of financial resources? When principals take time from their day and provide substitutes so that teachers have time to have a conversation with the administrative team, the significance of these conversations about each student's achievement is tremendously enhanced in the school culture. This cultural shift carries with it the commitment by teachers and administrators to support students.

5. Can I have Compelling Conversations in *content areas* that are not my expertise?

The focus of the scheduled conversation is the student, not the subject. Compelling Conversations provide a closer look at each child's progress by slowing down and taking time to discuss, without disruptions or interruptions, the needs of each child. The most current understanding of the instructional leader's role, as described by Robbins and Alvy (2004), includes the need to observe students while they are engaged in work and to observe the teacher's delivery system. Both are important leadership components, but observing teachers from the outside-in does not provide the inside perspective. As colleagues, the teacher and administrative team share different perspectives as their unique areas of expertise merge. Through backward mapping, each child's progress—beginning with the previous teacher's recommended levels, expectations for the child, and expectations of the teacher and administrative team—becomes a commitment. Content-specific questions are minimal because the purpose of the conversation is continuity of student progress in the particular grade level and between grade levels. This is the groundwork for sustainability (Chapter 4).

6. Are teachers uncomfortable with the *questions generated* during Compelling Conversations?

Just as apprehension accompanies most changes, teachers wondered what the real purpose of our conversations was. One teacher specialist explained, "Did you realize that some teachers are doing more informal assessments now?"

"Why?" I asked.

"Because they want to bring them to their conversations." Holding conversations with the administrative team can be motivational.

Gradually, trust increased. The Trust in Schools research (Byrk & Schneider, 2002) delineates the important relationship between relational trust, or social exchanges of schooling, and positive student achievement. Their research documents a strong statistical link between improvements in relational trust and gains in academic productivity. Kendra Trail, a principal from Pennsylvania, explained after having Compelling Conversations, "The improved trust factor that is developed between teacher and administration is amazing." Active listening plays a key role in developing relational trust. Genuine listening is a key skill for Data Team leaders as they pose questions and communicate student progress. As trust expands throughout a culture (Schnorr & Piercy, 2000), conversations become a mutually rewarding and beneficial learning opportunity for all participants. Lambert (2003) describes this kind of dialogue as being at the Teacher Leadership level.

As our teacher and administrator roles merged, uniting purpose with passion, the quest for student success reached a laser-like focus in many cases. Ignited with enthusiasm, our conversations could not be contained within the time frame for our meetings. Lambert (2003) explains this exceptional synergy that arises from conversations as "liminality," which occurs when traditional roles are dropped and we get to know ourselves and others in new ways, resulting in things never being quite the same again. Sharing ideas about bulletin boards has been replaced with conversations such as, "Did you hear about Anthony and Maria in second grade? They are also reading on grade level and it's only January. Let's find out what changes those teachers are making in instruction to meet the needs of our special education students!" Spilling over into the hallways and the faculty room, teachers continue questioning themselves and others.

Increased understanding resulted from returning to my very first question: *"Why are students who have no identified disabilities reading up to two years below their enrolled grade level?"* The answer to that question in most schools remained buried under generations of accepted practice that had become the norm. In contrast, accountability that is student-centered throws open the door of instructional decisions, inviting colleagues into vital, data-based conversations that expand teachers' capacity while diminishing the gap between student achievement and student potential.

Just as we must increase our success at holding onto student growth between grade levels, so that students are not dropped back in September, principals must establish improved student-centered accountability that is sustained beyond those principals' tenure within a school. Compelling Conversations shift the communication patterns, creating portals in the school culture to support and sustain change, as discussed in Chapter 4.

How to Conduct Compelling Conversations

The numerous long-term and positive results of regularly scheduled Compelling Conversations include increased student achievement (as measured by school,

◎◎
EXHIBIT 1.11   **Three Stages of Compelling Conversations**

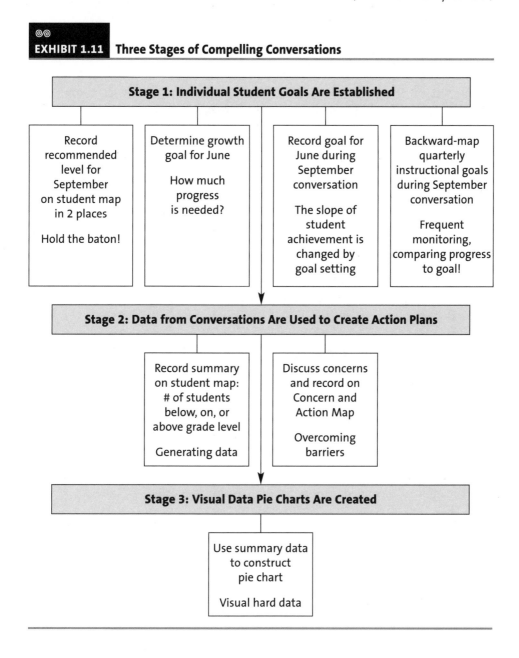

district, and state assessments), higher school-based standards, and the development of a strong collaborative culture that embraces student-centered accountability. The three immediate, direct stages of Compelling Conversations (see Exhibit 1.11) that provide the groundwork for these results are:

1. Goals that are established for every student by backward-mapping on the student map

2. Hard data that are transferred immediately from conversations for use by teachers, administrative teams, and Data Teams

3. Data snapshots that tell the ongoing story of accountability for each student, teacher, grade, and school

Stage 1: Individual Student Goals Are Established

Goals are backward-mapped on the student map (see Exhibits 1.12 and 1.13) during the first Compelling Conversation, which typically is held in September. The first conversation provides baseline data and establishes individual student goals that are monthly or for the marking period. Bernhardt supports this concept by stating, "Classroom teachers would benefit from having a database that would allow them to track student progress toward standards attainment throughout the year" (2002, p. 74).

The student map has multiple columns for data. These columns, which represent student progress, are completed during the Compelling Conversations as follows:

1. Last Reading Level Completed

This column, for last year's end-of-year outcome data, is considered historical data (Bernhardt, 2002). The column is titled to represent the type of data being recorded at a specific school, and filled in by this year's teacher. How is each student's outcome data from the previous year acquired? It is recorded on the student map (which can be in electronic format) from the previous year. When electronic files are used, it is most efficient if students' names are organized by the current year's reading/achievement group rather than alphabetically.

Recording the previous end-of-year outcome on the student map ensures that the current teacher has all the previous year's data available to establish a direct connection between the grade levels. Last year's end-of-year outcome is not just a number on a sheet, but a summary of cumulative achievement over time. This prevents the baton of student achievement from being dropped between grade levels.

EXHIBIT 1.12 **Student Map – Middle / Elementary**

Teacher: _____ **School Year:** 200___ – 200___

Incoming Students	Incoming State Reults	Last Year's Teacher Recommendations	1st Quarter	2nd Quarter	3rd Quarter	4th Quarter	State GOAL	Projected State Results	Teacher Recommendation

Number of students performing at Mastery or Above: ___

Number of students performing Below Mastery: ___

*Invisible Excellence Students

◎◎
EXHIBIT 1.13 **Student Map – Elementaries**

Group Students	Last Level		Sept	Nov	Jan	April	June Projected GOAL	Recommendations
	Completed Last Year	Recommended for this Year						

SUMMARY STATEMENTS:

Total number of my students receiving instruction *on or above* grade level now is: ____ ____ ____ ____ ____

Total number of my students receiving instruction *below* grade level now is: ____ ____ ____ ____ ____

*Invisible Excellence Students

Of course, the black hole that absorbs student growth over the summertime must be addressed. I ask teachers, "If students demonstrated that they knew and understood this information last year, do they no longer know it? Or would it be helpful to assess strategies and skills to determine specific weak areas that require review?"

ZOOMING IN ON SUCCESS

Why are these data so powerful? One teacher, Betsy Cunningham, explains: "This gives you an accurate place to start the year where you can rely on last year's information. I always do my own assessments and if there is a discrepancy, I check with last year's teacher. If I did not have this [student map] guide, I would not realize on the first day of school that some of these students were there [at a particular level]. This guide is helpful because this is the growth they made. They are there. Everything I am doing this year will be taken seriously by next year's teacher. The third-grade teacher cannot say, 'Oh, I am just going to begin teaching this student at a different level of instruction.' This is very valid because I can rely on last year's information." (Validity results from the fact that the data displayed on the student map are based on formal and informal assessments, confirmed through Compelling Conversations, and reflected in grades recorded on report cards.) "Without this, gaps are created. It helps the school culture because you are accountable."

Conversations data secure the continuation of steady growth for each student as he or she proceeds through the significant, formative years of education.

2. Recommended Reading Level to Begin This Year

This column contains data from the previous year's school records and student maps. The same reading level that last year's teacher put in the "Recommended Reading Level" column is recorded again under "September." Is this repetitive? Intentionally so. A pivotal point about the validity of holistic accountability is made each time a student's *end-of-year achievement level* is linked to the *beginning of next year's recommended level.*

Seeing and entering both the "Recommended" level to begin and the "September" beginning level, in a side-by-side format, contradicts the widely accepted notion that "they forget everything over the summer!" Teachers may have to review specific skills for a few weeks, but this generally does not require that a student's entire instructional level be dropped by up to half a year.

3. June Projected Goal

This end-of-year column is where the June goal is collaboratively determined. This goal is arrived at during the first Compelling Conversation by posing the question, "By the end of this year, at what level do we want this student reading/performing successfully?" The teacher and administrative team consider the amount of growth needed for the student to achieve one year's progress. Conversations include raising standards, particularly for students who would benefit from being above level and students who need to make more growth to achieve grade-level expectations. This is also referred to as the *annual yearly progress (AYP) goal.* The end-of-year outcomes/standards for each grade level will vary by district and state depending on the particular benchmarks required by state expectations. Examples of measurable end-of-year reading performance outcomes that can be backward-mapped from June (in September) include guided reading levels or reading basal levels. "Setting a standard helps us to diagnose achievement of individual students and our programs in order to understand strengths and weaknesses in our school" (Bernhardt, 2002, p. 73).

Why is recording reading levels on which the teacher is delivering instruction an appropriate measure of achievement? The point where students' eyes meet the page is where the accurate test of successful transfer of reading proficiency resides. At that point, a teacher's decision can greatly affect a child's future. "Students get a good start in school by leaving 1st grade with the ability to read at grade level" (Schmoker, 1999, p. 35). When students do not achieve this, efforts must remain focused on their gaining the ability to read and comprehend texts across the curriculum on grade level.

Internal measures such as reading levels increase teachers' direct connections with student achievement. One middle school teacher asked as she began backward-mapping June goals on the student map, "Do I have to sign this?" A personal hallmark moment of accountability resulted for this teacher, as entering each student's goal made those goals real.

4. Goals to Be Monitored During the Year

After determining the beginning and end-of-year achievement levels, the teacher and administrative team backward-map the individual student achievement outcome goal for each column according to month or marking quarter, beginning with June, for example, then *backing up* to April, January, November, and lastly to September. Each column is a measurable achievement goal, which will become the focus of the next Compelling Conversation. Marzano's research review reveals that the impact of setting goals on student achievement "ranges from a low of 18 percentile points to a high of 41 percentile points" (2003, p. 35). This makes *challenging goals* one of the five researched school-level factors that affect student achievement.

Because the majority of students are grouped with others who are performing at a similar level of proficiency, much of the backward mapping of goals goes quickly. The groupings are determined through evaluation of formal and informal measures of individual student achievement by the previous year's teachers and administrative teams. Students in a reading group have the same measurable outcome goals. The goals for the group are recorded. However, it is important to have individual students listed for each group, so that the progress of every student is captured, each child's needs are addressed as soon as they appear, and the student can be followed through the years. This prevents a student from getting "lost." There are no cracks that students can fall into, because every student's progress is reviewed during the school year. Technology templates assist the continuous flow of data. However, the lack of a district-wide data network should not prevent a principal from getting started with holding data-based conversations about student performance.

Once the goals are determined, the administrative team and the teacher discuss how to reach those goals, through a reflective conversation. Conversations during the backward-mapping process are focused on the needs of students and teachers. The "Compelling Conversations Coaching Questions" (Exhibit 1.14), based on Habits of Mind concepts (Costa & Kallick, 2000), support the principal and administrative team with reflective questions that can guide the conversation.

Goals for some students require additional support and strategies that extend beyond current identification practices. These strategies are mapped out in the "Concern and Action Map" described in Stage 2.

A transformation occurs—with teachers as well as with their special-needs students—as everyone begins to believe in themselves. Every teacher and each student recognizes that he or she is an important part of reaching goals successfully (see Chapter 3).

▪▪ What if a group of students requires growth to *exceed* the current grade level?

When students begin the school year above grade level, that excelled level is to be maintained in the backward-mapping process; in addition, potential additional growth must be considered during the year. Students also need to achieve their potential as it is identified during the school year. Backward-mapped goals should be flexible enough to encourage additional growth as evidenced in students' work

◉◉
EXHIBIT 1.14 **Compelling Conversations Coaching Questions**

BEGINNING OF YEAR:

1. What was this student's or group's last completed level last year? (See student map)
2. Where did last year's teacher *recommend* that this student begin? (See student map)
3. Are there any recommendations for students from last year's teacher that you do not consider accurate?
    When the answer is yes, the teacher and an administrator must address concerns with last year's teacher, face-to-face, for trust to be built and enhanced. This is of paramount importance if student-centered accountability is to prevail.
4. At what level *are you beginning* instruction for this student or group? (You do not lose a child when these two levels are the same.)
    - What do the data say?
    - How do the data support your decision?
5. At the end of the year, what is your projected performance-level goal for this student or group?
6. Some students need *more* than one year's growth to be performing on grade level. How much more progress, beyond one year, can this student make with you this year? How can I help you in achieving this goal?

To achieve this June's goal, let's backward-map this projected performance-level goal for each quarter.

7. What is the total number of students in your class on or above their enrolled grade level? How many are below the standard?
    (EXAMPLE: 19 students on or above, 6 students below. These figures are recorded each quarter on the student map. Later, these data are shared during Data Team meetings and faculty meetings.)

DURING THE YEAR:

1. At what level are you delivering instruction to this student now?
2. What evidence do you have to support your decision?
    - How do you know that?
    - How do the data support your decision?
3. What new goals do you have for this student or group?
4. How do you suppose this child's life would be affected if we were able to help him or her perform proficiently?
5. How can we work together to make that happen?
6. I see that these particular students *are not making progress* toward their goals. It looks like they are not going to make one year's progress.
    - What barriers do you see?
    - How can I help remove any barriers?
7. Are there students who are not making progress toward one full year's growth at this time?
    - Who are they?
    - For each student, what different modifications would help this student perform proficiently?

EXHIBIT 1.14   Compelling Conversations Coaching Questions *(continued)*

8. How will you know when progress increases?
9. If you could start this quarter all over, what would you do differently?
10. How can you make that happen in this new quarter?
11. What does this tell you?
12. What are you doing to ensure that your "advanced" (above grade level) students are being challenged?
    - How can we provide additional support for you and these students?
13. What are you doing to ensure that your students who are on grade level are continuing successfully?
14. As you envision this next quarter, what do you plan to do first?
15. How can we help you get started?
16. What data would you need to help understand this child's barriers?
17. How can we help remove barriers that are preventing progress?
18. What are you doing to challenge your good performers?
19. Is there a way you could . . . ?
20. What did you do that caused so much growth?
21. What do you think might happen if we . . . ?
    - If so, what challenges do you see in making this happen?
22. How can we help you with these challenges?
23. How might you arrange your schedule or groups differently to create more time for these [*number of*] students?
24. How does the progress of your boys and girls compare?
25. What do you predict would happen if we tried . . . ?
26. Describe how this child's progress is going now.
27. What conclusion can you draw about how well this plan is going?

END OF YEAR:
1. At what level did this student or group complete [*subject (e.g., reading)*] with you this year?
2. How much growth did each student make? (See student map)
3. Where do you recommend beginning [*subject (e.g., reading)*] for next year? (See student map)
4. What do the data say? How do the data support your recommendation for next year?
5. What worked this year?
6. What would you do differently next year?
7. What would you like to learn more about?

during the school year. When students demonstrate achievement of the current standards, they need to have the opportunity to progress to advanced levels. These decisions are made during the year. They are recorded appropriately and may replace the initial quarterly goals. Chapter 4 discusses this in detail.

▪▪ What if the student needs to make *more* than one year's growth to achieve proficiency?

When students begin the year below grade level, they will need to achieve more than one year's growth. This directly plans for the deterioration of the bell curve (Reeves, 2004).

Yes. That's right. Not because a federal law told us so. It is the right thing to do because these students deserve a better chance. During the backward-mapping process, increase the expectation to more than one year under the June goal and backward-map it under each quarter through September by asking a question such as, "What level could Michael be performing on by the end of the year if he received all the support he needed?" The principal, as a contributing leader, collaborates with teachers so that together they can change the slope of student achievement—one child at a time. This information is provided to the Data Teams, which support teachers by determining cause data and recommending ways to "intervene with different methods of instruction" (Bernhardt, 2002, p. 74).

The student map is not about collecting more data; it goes deeper than numbers. Student achievement of these goals during the school year means that a child has been guided and connected with his or her potential. Marzano (2003, p. 35) explains that Lipsey & Wilson's research on academic goals (1993) demonstrates that students learn best when expectations are clear.

Establishing a higher goal is half the battle (Exhibit 1.15). For example, at our school, the percentage of exiting special education students who achieve proficiency on the Maryland school assessment is 95.3 percent. The percentage of gifted students in our school is at the county average. Special education students are included in conversations in which we regularly make specific and accurate decisions. We must be equally accountable for these students because *these kids lives do matter.*

Exhibit 1.16 provides examples of noninstructional areas of need that have prevented students from succeeding. Students needing instructional support are discussed and next steps are recorded on the Concern and Action Map. Before we recommend a student to the Student Support Team, or for special education testing, we implement double-instructed reading when appropriate (as discussed in Chapter 3).

◎◎
EXHIBIT 1.15 **Student Map (with Sample Data)**

NOTE: The data included in this sample student map represent reading basal levels (in numerical form) and guided reading levels (in letter form). Any district or school data can replace the basal or guided reading data to establish higher student goals.

Group Students Gr. 2 Ms. Immler	Last Level Completed Last Year	Recommended for this Year	Sept	Nov	Jan	April	June Projected GOAL	Recommendations
GROUP 1:	2,1-K	2.1-L	2.1-L	2.2-M	2.2-M	3.2-O	3.2-O	3.2-P [1 year's progress]
Bennett, Charlotte								
Cato, Everett		IEP speech, writing						
Desmond, James								
Fitts, Sarah		new this year						
Gaynor, Ellen								
Glick, Jose								
Hardesty, Deion								
Rush, Nola								
South, Helen								
GROUP 2:	1.2-I	2.1-J	2.1-J	2.1-K	2.2-L	2.2-M	2.2-M	3.1-N [1 year's progress]
Bartz, Raphael								
Brown, Alvin								
Desmarais, Edwin		gifted program						
Foley, Lucinda								
Frye, Dwayne		counseling support						
Goode, Lola								
Magaha, Nick								
GROUP 3:		Primer-F	Pr.-F	1.2-H	2.1-J	2.2-L	2.2-L	2.2-M [1½ years' progress—INVISIBLE EXCELLENCE!]
Guarino, Harold		IEP & DIR	Pr.-F	1.2-H	2.1-J	2.2-L	2.2-L	
Kallenborn, Virginia		Tested Sp.Ed-DIR	Pr.-F	Pr.-F	1.2-I	2.1-K	2.2-L	
Lipscomb, Inga		IEP & DIR	Pr.-F	Pr.-F	1.2-I	2.1-K	2.2-L	
Molina, Mary		DIR	Pr.-F	1.2-H	2.1-J	2.2-L	2.2-M	Move up to 3.1-N
Romero, Robert		DIR	Pr.-F	1.2-H	2.1-J	2.2-L	2.2-L	
Snyder, Fred		New, DIR	Pre-p.	Pr.-F	1.2-I	2.1-J	2.1-K	2.2-L

SUMMARY STATEMENTS:

Total number of my students receiving instruction *on or above* grade level now is: 16 16 16 16 17

Total number of my students receiving instruction *below* grade level now is: 6 6 6 6 5

◎◎ EXHIBIT 1.16   Matching Area of Need with Action

Student's Name _____   Teacher's Name _____   Date _____

Area of Need	Plan for Action	Person Responsible
Unfinished homework	Meet with counselor each AM before school or before dismissal	Counselor
Lack of motivation	Team-teach one lesson per week for one month	Principal, reading specialist, special education teacher(s)
Gender-gap concern	Enrich current unit by researching and reporting through incorporating technology	Gifted and Talented teacher, media specialist, classroom teacher
Attendance	Shoot hoops in AM with assistant principal, principal, counselor, or physical education teacher Parent conference Walk track with counselor or leadership team member in AM	Assistant principal, principal, classroom teacher, counselor, physical education teacher, leadership team member
Overall unhappiness	Initiate dialogue by engaging in high-interest area with technology group	Media specialist, leadership team member
Notebook organization	Meet with counselor before dismissal	Counselor
Family issues, divorce Friendship problems	Schedule targeted groups for specific counseling support	Counselor

Stage 1 is completed when students' end-of-year goals have been backward-mapped during the first Compelling Conversation. Exhibit 1.17 can be used to have goal conferences with individual students. The results are then transferred into hard data, which is Stage 2.

⊚⊚
EXHIBIT 1.17 **Compelling Conversations Individual Student's Map**

Compelling Conversations Individual Student's Map for _____

Teacher:	School Year: 200__ – 200__			
Subject: Student:	1st Quarter	2nd Quarter	3rd Quarter	4th Quarter

To achieve my goals for this year, I will focus on making progress every marking period.

To improve at this time, I am willing to commit to doing the following:

Student's Signature _____

Teacher's Signature _____

Stage 2: Data from Conversations Are Used to Create Action Plans

To meet the needs of students who are not achieving adequate progress, a Concern and Action Map (Exhibit 1.18) for each teacher is collaboratively developed during Compelling Conversations. The purpose of the map is to provide an avenue of support in addition to the standard interventions. The Concern and Action Map incorporates every available resource that a principal and school have access to. It does *not* resemble an individual education plan (IEP) and is not intended to be an IEP. The action-plan concept is similar to other action plans currently being used in school systems, as its purpose is to identify any voids or gaps that have become barriers to a student's progress. The Concern and Action Map does have additional potential because the identified student barriers and solutions become part of our individual Compelling Conversations, which intensify the focus.

◎◎
EXHIBIT 1.18 **Concern and Action Map (by Teacher)**

Teacher Name: _____   Year: _____

Student's Name	Area of Concern	September Actions	November Actions	January Actions	April Actions	June Results
1.						
2.						
3.						
4.						
5.						

Some students need to achieve more than one year's growth. The Concern and Action Map also documents the next steps the teacher or administrative team will take, as determined during the conversations, to meet the needs of such students. These data will be shared with the Data Teams, as described in Chapter 2.

Hard data are an outcome of the first Compelling Conversation and every monthly/marking-period conversation after that. After completing Stage 1, backward mapping to set goals, the second immediate task is to transform Compelling Conversations into formative hard data. All conversations result in hard data for the teacher and the Data Team to compare to the formative goals for each month or marking period. Schmoker emphasizes the significance of outcomes thus: "We have seen how teams benefit from a clear focus on goals" (2001, p. 41). Compelling Conversations will result in the following monthly/marking-period outcomes:

▪▪ Job-embedded hard data about every student's end-of-year goal

- Job-embedded hard data about every student
- Each student's actual progress toward his or her goal during the year
- The teacher's entire-class performance level
- The total team's performance level
- The entire school's level of performance

The data are generated with the question that begins every Compelling Conversation focused on reading improvement: *"At what instructional level are you delivering instruction successfully to this student?"* These data are recorded on the student map, which is contrasted with the previously determined goals as indicated with reading levels.

The student's instructional level is what is recorded on the student map. An assessment score could be recorded instead of the instructional level. However, the *instructional level* means the level at which the student can make progress in reading with instructional guidance. Reading level, or the performance information that is reported, is based on success indicated with hard data collected from formal and informal assessments and student work that has been evaluated; thus, it better represents the learner. Making decisions based on a student's instructional performance or level provides teams with informative conversation data that are not limited to assessment scores, because multiple forms of information are integrated into the instructional level.

The teacher is the most accurate data source and indicator of a student's current progress. Teachers' understanding of each student's sustained performance exceeds the meaning of a single number, acquired from a list of questions designed by a group of people working outside the school community. Therefore, the Compelling Conversation Framework (see Exhibit 1.19) is used to support the teacher in generating authentic data for each student by posing clear questions about basic teacher instructional decisions.

The Compelling Conversation Framework can be referred to when initiating conversations with the faculty. The response to the key question "At what instructional level are you delivering instruction successfully to this student (based on what you expect this student to know and be able to do)?" provides a point of inquiry that goes directly to the heart of accountability. The response to this question requires the teacher to know each student's daily performance and to determine the appropriate instructional level. This level is based on previous successful assessment results. It is the unique teacher expertise, acquired during education courses in college, in-services, workshops, professional reading, experience, and collaboration, that comes to bear upon this crucial question.

EXHIBIT 1.19 **Compelling Conversations Framework**

> **Basic Framework for Understanding: At what level are you delivering instruction successfully to this student?**

- What evidence (formative assessment) do you have that this student is learning successfully at this level?

- What are you doing to ensure that your ADVANCED students are being challenged?
  - □ What can we do to help?
  - □ How could we provide additional support for you and your advanced students?

- What are you doing to ensure that students who are performing ON grade level are continuing successfully?

- Are there any students who are NOT making independent progress toward one full year's growth, based on the recommendations of last year's teacher, at this time?

- What are you doing for students who are performing BELOW grade level to help them achieve *more* than one year's growth?
  - □ What can we do to help?
  - □ How could we provide additional support for you and your students who are performing BELOW grade level?

Total number of my students receiving instruction *on or above* grade level now is: _____

Total number of my students receiving instruction *below* grade level now is: _____

TERMS:

BELOW—A student who is receiving instruction that is NOT ON his or her enrolled grade level

ON—A student who is receiving instruction at his or her enrolled grade level

ABOVE—A student who is receiving instruction one or more years ahead of his or her enrolled grade level

To ask this question of teachers is to honor them. Inherent in this question is the belief that the teacher is central to a child's success. As a principal who spent nearly two decades as a teacher, I passionately hold this belief to be a core truth. It is because of esteem for every teacher that our conversations begin with their decisions about the instructional level for each child.

Working through the Conversation Framework

By posing the question, "At what instructional level are you delivering instruction successfully to this student," you are creating a point at which the teacher can respond with measurable data. Achievement of the monthly/marking-period student goals is the focus. See Exhibit 1.14 for additional coaching questions.

The hard data recorded on the student map *are* the current instructional level. The dialogue in the conversation focuses on the level of instruction where the student is currently learning. For example, in third grade, a basal reader level might be 3.1. A guided reading level could be 26. In middle school the level might be Lexile 960. Record this number on the classroom student map in whatever way your school district determines reading instructional levels. Each marking period, the current level of instruction is compared with the previously recorded student goal, set during the backward-mapping process in the first conversation.

> *At what level are you delivering instruction to this child today? As the teacher, where do you see this student as a learner? These are the responsible questions because the sole focus is accountability.*

Enter the final data for each conversation (including the first) at the bottom of the student map. The following teacher responses become the data pie chart for the teacher, which is Stage 3.

The number of my students receiving reading instruction *on* and *above* grade level for this month/marking period is: _____.

The number of my students receiving instruction *below* grade level for this month/marking period is: _____.

Follow-Up Monthly/Marking-Period Conversations

Conversations revisit the student's goals for that time period. The initial conversation and student map constructed in September are used as reference points for monitoring the goals in subsequent conversations. When meeting with teachers to confer about students' progress, use the framework of questions to reflect upon the process to date. As you will see in Exhibit 1.20, we revisit the goals, discuss any barriers to achieving those goals, and end by once again writing in numbers those students who are achieving below, on, and above grade level at that time.

We have data from the conversations about the following:

■▪ Each student's actual progress toward his or her goals during the year

EXHIBIT 1.20 Flow Map for Compelling Conversations

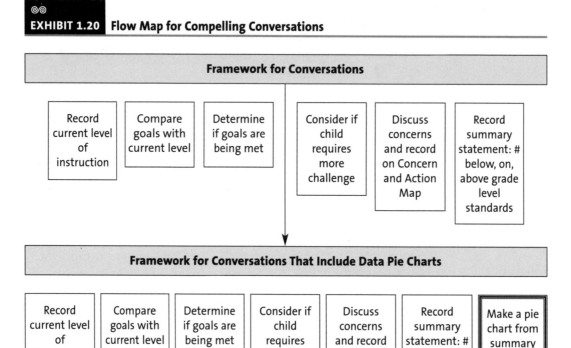

- The teacher's entire-class performance level for the month/marking period
- The total team's performance level for the month/marking period
- The entire school's performance level for the month/marking period

Powerful results of Compelling Conversations that extend beyond the data are discussed in Chapter 4.

What If the Student Did Not Make the Projected Progress?

The first conversation began with the end in mind (McTighe & Wiggins, 1999), by backward-mapping from June to set the monthly/marking-period goals for each student. When a student does not achieve the goal indicated on the student map, proceed with additional inquiry-based reflection, using the questions from the framework, to determine the causes and to plan for success:

- "I noticed here that Isabel did not achieve her goal. What would she need to make this happen?"

- "What do you need from us to provide Isabel the best opportunity to learn?"

- "What modifications should we make to her Concern and Action Map?

At first, I posed such questions with trepidation because the answer would require my commitment, in advance, to an unknown. That is no longer a concern because where would these children be without our total dedication to help them succeed? My teachers know that I nearly always say, "Yes, I can do that for you," and then figure out how later. How can I put myself in that position of accountability? Teachers do every day. Putting my word on the line for them means a lot. Sharing accountability means that we discuss the interventions that would overcome the students' barriers—and then I make every effort to locate resources to enable those interventions.

Are teachers afraid to be honest since I am also responsible for evaluating them? It depends on the level of trust. Byrk and Schneider's research on trust in schools explains, "Actions principals play a key role in developing and sustaining relational trust. Principals establish both respect and personal regard when they acknowledge the vulnerabilities of others and actively listen to their concerns" (2002, p. 137). Conversations provide the context for expansion of these qualities. When teachers know that you are passionate about students' learning, and when passion is mutual, there is no threat because accountability is equally shared. There is no blame when collaboration is genuine.

Discomfort can arise for a teacher if an action plan has been implemented and the principal has provided every resource necessary, but the student does not achieve any growth and the teacher still indicates that growth occurred. This is the purpose of the question in Exhibit 1.19: "What evidence (formative assessment) do you have that this student is learning successfully at this level?" Occasional aberrations may occur until the process has been implemented for the first year. The bottom line is that teachers directly commit to their recommendations for next year's placement level on the student maps, done during our last conversation and provided to the next grade's teachers. Recommendations must be supported with standard classroom and district assessments so that the next teacher will be able to continue instruction with full confidence that the recommendation was accurate; in this way, accountability for each student's achievement is honestly and accurately passed to the next grade. To be less than honest or accurate is to jeopardize personal credibility with colleagues and the administrative team. Having accuracy embedded is a significant aspect of what drives accountability with Compelling Conversations.

Expectations for each and every child are dramatically clear. Most importantly, leadership's expectations establish the standard for the school. Perhaps you are wondering, "How can I be a reflection of a standard?" Your personal standards are identified when you ask yourself the question, "What do I stand for? What am I about?"

Student progress is one example of a standard-based core value that can guide your course as a leader and affect all students within your care. The association between you and what you represent to your staff has to be clear. For example, long before the federal government initiated the No Child Left Behind requirements, I had always believed that "a year for a year" is the minimum expectation for every child's academic progress. Every child deserves a year's growth for a year's time in school. Should that be increased for high-achieving students, to ensure that they are reaching their potential? Absolutely. Marzano explains, "Opportunity to learn has the strongest relationship with student achievement of all school factors" (2003, p. 22). As noted in effective-school research (Lezotte & McKee, 2002), below-grade-level students require more than one year's growth to eventually perform at proficiency. The significance of "expectation" research is that "setting academic goals for all students that do not underestimate their potential" is important (Marzano, 2003, p. 18). The following conversation shows how having high expectations and Compelling Conversations can build trust.

 ## ZOOMING IN ON SUCCESS: HIGH SCHOOL

Principal/Leadership Team member: How have James and Harley been doing since our last conversation?

English Literature Teacher: I had James and Harley stay after class and I asked each of them to start meeting with me regularly, either in the morning before homeroom, or after school. James chose the morning because of his sports practice after school and Harley decided that he could find time to meet with me at lunch two or three times a week. During these meetings, I began the conversation by going over each boy's grades and asking him what grade he wanted to receive in the class. They both told me that they needed to pass the class to graduate, and that they wanted to make sure their grade would ensure their graduation. I told each of them that I would develop a contract with them and that if they followed through on the contract, I would guarantee that they would pass the class. However, they would have to live up to their end of this agreement.

Principal/LTM: That sounds like an interesting idea. Tell me about this "contract."

Teacher: First, I said I wanted them to come to class prepared each day, with their assignments read and their homework completed. Second, I wanted each boy to choose a person in the class to become his personal academic coach—someone who would help him with assignments in class and outside of class. They were both nervous about asking a classmate for help. I gave them the names of several students who are doing well. They both wanted to think this offer over, so I gave them until Friday after class to decide. They both decided to work with a classmate. This coaching, and their meetings with me, seem to be working.

Principal/LTM: James and Harley know how much you believe in them. They are making better decisions because they trust you.

Teacher: Talking with you about the students keeps me focused on what they are doing in class. I know we discuss the tough cases, but I can really keep my students on track when I think about how to best differentiate for their individual needs. Also, Brett and Harry are doing very well now, and they have really settled down since I moved them away from each other in my fourth-period class.

Principal/LTM: Keep up the great work and let me know what the team or I can do to help you. Our attendance numbers have steadily improved since I have taken the time to have these conversations with you and the other teachers. I also know which students need to be monitored closely, and I have staff from the guidance office and from my administrative team try to make contact with each of those students daily. These conversations cut down on behavior problems. Did you hear that on Monday, Jamal came to me and asked for help with a problem he was having with someone trashing his locker? Last month, I would have been the last to know, and it would have taken me half a day to sort out the problem. The conversations take time, but they are valuable.

Notice how the following inquiry-based conversation gently nudges expectations higher.

ZOOMING IN ON SUCCESS: ELEMENTARY SCHOOL

Principal/Leadership Team member: I see that that these three students are not making steady progress toward their goals. It looks like they're not going to achieve one year's progress.

Teacher: That's right. I don't think these three boys will be able to achieve the June goals we wrote on my student map in September.

Principal/LTM: What makes you believe this?

Teacher: I just do not think they can do it. They are not motivated, do not do their homework, do not complete their reading class work for comprehension—they just don't seem to care about anything.

Principal/LTM: Kaitlyn, it may be true that these boys cannot successfully achieve third-grade standards, *but we must believe that they can.* (Marzano explains, "Belief that hard work and determination—effort—will lead to success has the greatest effect on achievement. Believing in effort can serve as a powerful motivational tool that students can apply to any situation" [2001, p. 97].)

Now if we believe that they can succeed, what barriers would need to be overcome? Let's talk about class work. Do you think the boys would be motivated if they knew that every day before lunch you would give them each a pass to visit me in my office to talk about their work for the day? How about if I let each student select a mechanical pencil from our school store that they could take home after completing three consecutive assignments?

Teacher: That might help. But I have a different idea! I'll have them graph their progress in vocabulary and comprehension so they can compare the differences. I think if they could see that their vocabulary was visibly much stronger than their comprehension, they might want to try harder.

Principal/LTM: Okay! That's a better idea! Let me know if we need to try anything else.

Teacher: Okay, but I still would like for them to stop by to see you in the morning to show you their homework as soon as they get off the bus in the morning. Maybe that would motivate them to complete it at night.

Principal/LTM: Great! I'll look forward to seeing them in the morning.

Do you hear the unspoken core value driving the conversation with compelling commitment toward goals that are challenging and unrelenting?

Expectations.

Just three boys.

Could their lack of achievement have gone unnoticed before Compelling Conversations were instituted? Perhaps.

Did high expectations make a difference in their lives? Ask them! Then, look at their faces.

To support continuous student progress, articulation cards (see Exhibit 1.21) are used in many districts. Articulation cards, completed for each student by the

EXHIBIT 1.21   Articulation Card

ARTICULATION CARD

School Year 200__ – 200__   Student Name:

GRADE LEVEL: RELATED SERVICES:

Reading Teacher: Speech__
Last received instruction on ___ Reading Level   Language__
Begin instruction on ___ Guided Reading Level   DDR Tutor__
Recommended materials: EEP-Math__ Reading__
 Leveled readers __Below __On __Above

                                               ESOL _____ intervention
                                               Referred-Intervention
                                                 Committee (IC)__
Literature/Trade Books: Special Ed__ 504__

Writing:
____ Dependent
____ Progressing
____ Independent
____ Elaborates
____ Includes details
____ Uses mechanics

Math Teacher:
 September___ January___ June___
Receives instruction
____ Above grade level
____ On grade level
____ Modified program

teacher at the end of the year, contain a summary of pertinent information. These cards are provided to next year's teachers for easy access to an array of vital data. They are not needed for Compelling Conversations, and are not a component of the process, but they are helpful records for teachers to have. Articulation cards are used in our district to help streamline access to multiple pieces of data and to ensure that all the data get into the hands of teachers. How many more times do we need to ask about a child's test scores and hear a teacher reply, "I don't know. I haven't had time to check their files"? No wonder. Although some data are accessible through electronic means, other individual student data are usually stored in locked confidential files, the office cumulative files, or stored in the principal's state files. Data should flow through a school, between grade levels, and among special areas as naturally as a river winds along its course, without the debris of summer interruptions.

Organizing Student Maps

When hard copies of the student maps for each teacher and grade are desired, copies in the form of a notebook can become a much-used resource for teams and administrators in the school. This notebook of student maps is used by:

- Special education teachers and reading specialists, to monitor, at a glance, the progress of all the students they work with in relation to the regular or general education population
- Reading specialists and administrators, to determine the best placements for new students
- Administrators, to refer to during walk-throughs and observations and to use for observing students' progress in comparison to their goals
- Administrators, to field parents' questions about students' progress
- Administrators, to know, at a glance, the actual progress made by each child during the year

In communications with parents, percentages and standardized scores are not informative. The student maps provide actual reading progress, during the entire year, by the levels used within your district.

 ZOOMING IN ON SUCCESS

Just yesterday a parent called because she was concerned that her daughter seemed weak in reading. I immediately referred to the teacher's student map for the year. I assured this student's mom that throughout the year her daughter had demonstrated steady progress in reading and was recommended to begin fifth-grade reading on grade level. The Concern and Action Plan had a clear recommendation for next year. I added that we had already planned at our last conversations meeting to begin the next year with some additional, informal support to maintain her daughter's growth and confidence.

This mother was overwhelmed that I knew her daughter's progress—not in empty percentages from a state assessment report, but actual reading progress for the entire year. Because it was summertime and teachers were not there to consult with, I felt gratified to have been able to help. This parent's appreciation was so profound that I was reminded once again that being a contributing leader means being an active collaborator who participates directly in achievement. When accountability is student-centered, it is accurate, constructive, and easily communicated to parents.

As one teacher noted, "Our Compelling Conversations data were essential in helping my team identify struggling learners, identify specific areas of concern, and identify specific strategies and interventions that enabled these learners to be more successful."

Compelling Conversations make continuous progress measurable with hard data. Continuity is the key factor, because goals that are based on instruction and supported with assessments provide stability in a world of ever-changing assessments. Michael Fullen expressed it best: "In schools, for example, the main problem is not the absence of innovations but the presence of too many disconnected, episodic, piecemeal, superficially adorned projects. Schools are suffering the additional burden of having a torrent of unwanted, uncoordinated policies and innovations raining down on them from hierarchical bureaucracies" (2001, p. 108). What an understatement! In most districts, teachers are expected to make aligned decisions to assure the flow of continuous progress for all students among six grade levels, based on five very different state, district, and school measures. Five different assessment measures for a single student moving through one school! We all deserve a sign: "Michael Fullen must have been here!"

The data generated in Stage 2 are used to make data pie charts for the teachers and their teams; these charts constitute Stage 3.

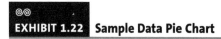

EXHIBIT 1.22 Sample Data Pie Chart

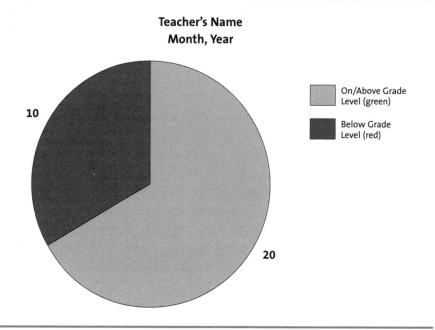

Teacher's Name
Month, Year

10

20

On/Above Grade
Level (green)

Below Grade
Level (red)

Stage 3: Visual Data Pie Charts Are Created

The third stage of Compelling Conversations is the transformation of data from the student map into a visual representation: a class pie chart of reading progress. Data snapshots, dramatic in simplicity, tell a story. The following details the process that generates data pie charts for the individual teachers.

The response to the question, "At what instructional level are you delivering instruction successfully to this student?," is totaled directly on the class student map. The *total* number of students currently receiving instruction below, on, and above their enrolled grade level appears on the bottom of the class student map.

These two responses are the data used to create simple pie charts (easy to generate when data are entered into Microsoft Excel). The data pie chart rolls out immediately for the teacher. One extra is made or copied for the school leader's data photo album (described in Chapter 2). Data pie charts (see Exhibit 1.22) are a natural next step after discussing the number of students reading above, on, and below grade level. Merging the roles of the leadership team and teacher has permitted us to look accountability in its black-and-white face and not see a monster.

Each number represents an individual student in this teacher's class. The transparency and transfer of data among administrators, teachers, and Data Teams provides timely opportunities to make modifications that result in students achieving their expected goals.

That's it. A concrete snapshot of data for each teacher to hold is a picture of progress for her or his class. It is also a picture of our Compelling Conversations about students resulting from the decisions that led to their success.

Later, this simple pie chart is included in a data photo album for the school and as the "next read" for Data Team pie charts for team goal setting, as described in Chapter 2. Though they are certainly not the whole story, data pie charts do provide a perspective for collaboration for leaders who aim to contribute to the success of all the students in the school. Our student population has exceeded 850, with more than 175 students per grade level, and grade-level teams of eight teachers, but the progress of each student has been condensed to one glance. These are real kids, color-coded in one of two colors: green for students who are receiving instruction on or above their enrolled grade level and red for students who are receiving instruction below their level.

How to Move Beyond Pie Charts

To be sure, these data are informative, but accountability contemplates more than a photo album of pie charts. It's time to move the data from the pie charts off the walls and into the bloodstream of instructional decisions and instructional models. When I was assigned to be its principal, 61 percent of the students at my school were not reading proficiently, according to the Maryland state assessment. What prevented our school's performance from improving (Senge, 1999) was that our achievement outcomes hit a large barrier that constrained progress: communication. It is quite likely that the high percentage of students reading below grade level had actually existed for some time. Until the root cause of low achievement was addressed, though, improvement was minimal.

To help our faculty concretely understand, I described our water-leakage problem in terms of a larger barrier, a *setpoint*. Every time it rained, a dozen ceiling tiles were replaced. This did not improve the water problem at all because our school's leakage problem had a much larger root cause that needed attention. Our building's setpoint was that new cement joints and sealant had to be applied to the exterior. The facilities department understandably delayed this expensive undertaking. However, setpoints do not just fade away! A few years ago, with new cement and sealant, our water problem was resolved.

Likewise, it was necessary to address the root cause of the poor communication that was our limit to growth. Compelling Conversations increase communication between the administrative team and teachers. The timely, internal results from these conversations are then used by Data Teams to help establish monthly and annual goals that are frequently monitored to support school achievement goals.

Summary

Compelling Conversations are an effective form of assessment and accountability for school leaders and teachers that improves student performance. Conversations, a dialogue between each teacher and the administrative team, include backward mapping of students' progress through the year to establish a schedule for students' needed gains (sometimes even more than a year's growth) within the school year. It is during the first conversation about the children that the commitment is made to change the slope of student performance *during* that year. This first conversation serves as the anchor point for monitoring student progress toward the determined annual goal at subsequent conversations throughout the year. The relationship between regularly scheduled conversations between the administrative team and teachers and increased learning is evidenced with triangulated state, district, and school data. Frequent monitoring of each student's achievement, based on the expected standards that were backward-mapped during the Compelling Conversations, generates data to support the work of Data Teams. These conversations augment the work of Data Teams by increasing teacher and student accountability, providing a means for supervision and evaluation, and providing a measurable type of formative student assessment that has predictive value as to high-stakes assessment results. Conversations lead to the development of an antecedent of success (White, 2005): a culture based on trust with optimal accountability that is not feared, but embraced as students' performance continuously improves.

The data generated during Compelling Conversations communicate the progress of individual students to the grade-level team. The use of data from Compelling Conversations to establish monthly team goals is discussed in Chapter 2.

CHAPTER 2

CONVERSATIONS: *The Shared Approach to Accountability*

Essential Question: *How can individual Compelling Conversations with teachers contribute to measurable Data Team goals?*

Chapter Foreword   DOUGLAS B. REEVES

"It's a great idea in theory, but I just don't have the time!" As a busy classroom teacher or school administrator, you know how fully these words resonate with your personal experience. Data analysis, accountability, and the Compelling Conversations described in these pages all sound fine in theory, but there are students clamoring for attention, parents demanding appointments, and endless administrative requirements. Although a consideration of individual student achievement data and thoughtful reflection on accountability are great ideas in theory, they must take a back seat to the exigencies of the moment.

Wait a moment. Compelling Conversations will *save* time. It is the gift every teacher and school leader needs: the gift of time to reflect and renew. Invest a few minutes in the following pages and you will learn how to focus instructional energy. In contrast to many data analysis plans, which drain your energy and time by perseverating on weaknesses, you will learn how to identify and focus on your strengths. Rather than waste time on district or building average scores, you will learn how to focus on the needs of individual students. Dr. Piercy will guide you through proven steps of analysis that have been effective in schools with a wide variety of demographic characteristics. For high-poverty schools, this process will encourage the discouraged. For schools with economically advantaged students, the steps of analysis and accountability in this chapter will challenge and stimulate teachers and administrators. Most importantly, you will learn how avoid analyzing only a sterile set of test scores and, instead, how to engage in a thoughtful conversation about teaching strategies, leadership decisions, and other adult actions that influence student achievement.

Drawing on a wide variety of research and vast personal experience, Dr. Piercy invites us into a Compelling Conversation that will improve achievement, reduce equity gaps, and—just as I promised—save time.

Introduction

The needs of the children who come into our schools today, and the needs of their families, contrast dramatically with the needs of those who walked the same path years ago. Even students of only five years ago seem fundamentally different from today's student population. What has remained the same is the hope for a life filled with potential, carried within the heart of the child entering school for the first time, sometimes alone. The bewildering convergences of technology, world events, and shifting enrollments have required teachers to run ever-faster just to stay in place. Although our country and our world have changed, the promise of education has not.

As we continue in an age of change and unfolding expectations, it is vital that individual teachers, principals, and school leaders communicate at all levels. Sharing responsibilities through collaboration supports schools as they attempt to adjust appropriately and effectively to current demands. Communication is the key component in setting and reaching productive student, teacher, and school goals. Teamwork is vital, both for providing opportunities for collaboration, and for collaboration itself about data that lead to better student achievement. The formation of Data Teams, developed by The Leadership and Learning Center (2006), establishes a collaborative framework that is structured with scheduled team meetings. Through the use of data-driven decision-making processes (CPA, 2004), these Data Teams focus on teaching and learning.

Make time to talk with your teachers regularly. These talks, and the compelling reflections they stimulate, cause teachers to think differently about their students. Conversations about higher standards for all students result in student goals gradually increasing. These goals are backward-mapped from June to September, based on the expectation that students will achieve at least one year's growth for each school year. "A year for a year" progress is built into the conceptual framework of public education's 12-year design and the curriculum standards set for each year. Nevertheless, this framework alone has not proven successful or adequate for all of today's children. The job-embedded data from Compelling Conversations, when shared with Data Teams, support students' achievement of one year's growth, and sometimes more if needed, in one school year.

Where does accountability begin?

The following stages briefly summarize how Compelling Conversations about student achievement are transferred into hard data (see Exhibit 2.1 and Chapter 1). This chapter details how these data are used by teams to establish yearly and monthly team goals.

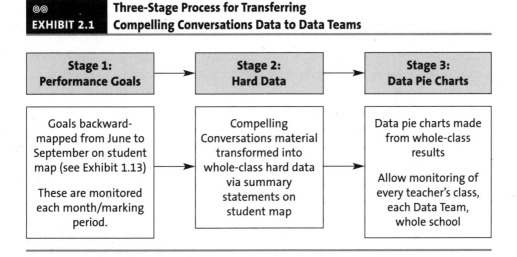

⊚⊚ **EXHIBIT 2.1**	**Three-Stage Process for Transferring Compelling Conversations Data to Data Teams**

Stage 1: Performance Goals	Stage 2: Hard Data	Stage 3: Data Pie Charts
Goals backward-mapped from June to September on student map (see Exhibit 1.13) These are monitored each month/marking period.	Compelling Conversations material transformed into whole-class hard data via summary statements on student map	Data pie charts made from whole-class results Allow monitoring of every teacher's class, each Data Team, whole school

Stage 1 of Compelling Conversations: Individual Student Goals Are Established

Goals are established in Stage 1, both for students who can achieve progress *beyond* their grade level and for students who need to make *more than one year's* progress just to be on level. These goals are set during the first conversation, held in September, between the principal or school leaders and teachers.

These student achievement/performance goals, monitored continuously throughout the year, are the focus of our conversations. Each Compelling Conversation culminates with the teacher generating direct summary statements about each student's progress for that quarter (used during Stage 2).

Stage 2 of Compelling Conversations:
Data from Conversations Are Used to Create Action Plans

Each Compelling Conversation with every teacher ends with the following summary statements:

> Teacher Summary Statements:
>
> Total number of my students receiving instruction on or above grade level now is: _____
>
> Total number of my students receiving instruction below grade level now is: _____

The total number of students for each response is written on the teacher's student map.

These statements constitute direct, honest, black-and-white hard data. The power of these particular data lies in their authenticity: the data are *generated directly* by the most expert source, the child's teacher. They are shared with the administrative team directly, and in pure numbers that represent real children, not percentages or averages. These children are in teachers' classrooms *at this time.*

The *instructional level* is the level at which the student can make progress with instructional guidance. This level is sometimes referred to as the *teaching level,* because the text to be read or other material to be mastered must be challenging, but not too difficult. Success here indicates that a student is learning and is able to transfer that learning with understanding. Instructional levels, determined by teachers, are informed with data from group discussions, actual student work, and assessments.

Data Team decisions that consider a student's instructional level in turn provide authentic data because the instructional level depends on the teacher's direct interaction with the student. Instructional levels provide continuity in the recording of a student's progress for kindergarten through grade 5 and middle school grades, because each grade incorporates some form of reading gradient or other level of student performance. These are determined by formative assessments of student achievement and other data on student proficiency that are more current and specific than the end-of-year district and state assessments. This is the performance level that is recorded on the student map. These are the Compelling Conversations data that are compiled and provided to the Data Team and included in the Data Team process (discussed later in this chapter).

Stage 3 of Compelling Conversations: Visual Data Pie Charts Are Created

The total number of students in the summary statement (from the teacher's student map) is transferred into data pie charts by typing the two responses—the number of students performing on/above the number performing below—into Microsoft Excel and printing out pie charts. One data pie chart (see Exhibit 2.2) is given to the teacher. Another copy, which includes each team member's pie-chart data and is sized to fit on one page, is given to the Data Team by the principal or school leader.

◎◎
EXHIBIT 2.2   **Sample Data Pie Chart**

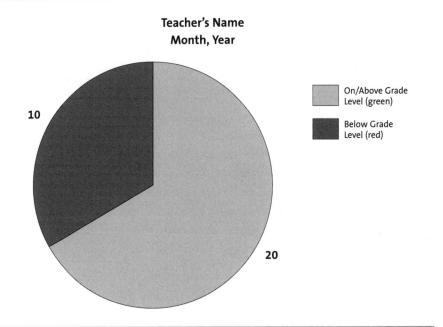

Teacher's Name
Month, Year

- On/Above Grade Level (green)
- Below Grade Level (red)

10

20

How often to use data pie charts is an individual leadership decision. More frequent use does inform team decisions. Still, the reality is that for data to be useful, it must be manageable, which explains why data-driven decision making is vital for student success. As Joe Torgesen from the U.S. Department of Education stated, "Data collection is not hard. What we *do* with data is hard" (Torgesen, 2004). The use of data is enhanced with team collaboration.

When students are struggling, you know who they are.

From Individual to Collaborative Decisions

Just as the success of a war cannot be determined by body count, leadership success is not measured by test scores. When the school leadership uses data to increase communication throughout a culture, the outcomes are visible far beyond the walls of displayed data. The success is evident in the potential being realized in students' lives.

The unfortunate norm, inherent in the traditional organizational structure of schools, is individual teachers making decisions that are not communicated to other teachers, either within their teams or to teachers at different grade levels. The problem of *no one understanding why* some students were reading below their grade level (see Chapter 1) arose from the fact that those decisions were made in previous grades. The breakdown of communication between grade levels about students, and the data that represent them, is a flaw embedded in the history of America's schools. This is accepted practice, but not acceptable, as evidenced in the following example:

> When I was a classroom teacher, I recall my principal handing everyone on our team a folder marked, "California Test of Basic Skills." He explained that although the state assessments were not that meaningful, we should take a look at them. When he left the room, we opened our individual folders containing our class results. No, we did not put each of our folders on the table in open view of our colleagues. Our conversation centered on the accepted excuse, "Tests never test what we teach." This isolated decision-making model directly contrasts with the collaborative communication in Data Teams.

When teachers share their class data with a Data Team and the team members support one another with suggestions, transparency in decisions is created. This transparency leads to informed decisions about students.

Conditions for Success

School systems are accountable for an ever-swelling number of student variables that are also increasing in intensity. Against this background, Douglas Reeves (2004) and Mike Schmoker (2001) have led the direction schools must take to support student achievement. Reeves and Schmoker have provided a balance of belief systems, processes to guide us, and support documents to immediately transfer concepts into our schools.

Communication is fundamental in shaping organizational behavior and practices, and improvement in communication results in willingness of teachers to *share all data* comfortably within Data Teams. Schmoker believes that "[w]hen teachers regularly and collaboratively review assessment data for the purpose of improving practice to reach measurable achievement goals, something magical happens" (2001, p.1). To initiate and support Data Team communication, it is first necessary to consider time.

> *Data Team conversations are powerful, continuous, and formative conversations about data.*

Making Time for Data Teams

Time for Data Teams to meet is the first factor that must be addressed if teams are to be successful in communicating about the improvement of student learning. A significant leadership task is creating team time. Especially when team size prevents common planning, time must be creatively carved out of the standard day.

Data Team Time "On the Clock"

The following suggestions for creating time for Data Teams within a regular school day are in addition to those recommended by The Leadership and Learning Center, formerly Center for Performance Assessment:

- **Data Team Time Lunch Hours: One-hour lunches**
  Request the local library to present a 30-minute storytelling program to each grade level immediately following that grade's 30-minute lunch period. (Public libraries frequently offer storytelling as a free service.) Connecting the storytelling half-hour to the lunch half-hour creates a "Data Team Time Lunch Hour."
  Try to schedule one storytelling each marking period. When possible, order pizza for teams on this day to add to the excitement!

- **Cultural Program Team Time: 45 minutes for Data Teams**
  When special programs are presented, try to schedule them twice: once in the morning and once in the afternoon, to reduce the size of the audience to a manageable number. This way the principal and assistant principal, along with instructional assistants, can supervise the students. This creates a 45-minute block for Data Teams. Backing this block up to lunch (especially if lunch can occasionally be ordered out) gives Data Teams the *option* of taking an additional 30 minutes, for a total of 1 hour and 15 minutes.

- **Mondays at MAE: 30 minutes weekly team time for professional development**
  "Mondays at <u>M</u>t. <u>A</u>iry <u>E</u>lementary" (MAE; substitute your school's initials)

is time created *weekly* for team professional development. Also, central office representatives request time to speak during most faculty meetings, so schedule these speakers during this time frame to preserve faculty meetings for Data Teams. The professional development can be team-specific or for all grades. Examples of topics that expand teacher capacity during professional development team time are:

- Professional reading study groups
- Differentiation of Instruction Strategies
- Habits of Mind: Integration into Instruction
- Integrating Technology for Reading and Math Instruction
- Find the Data Treasure Hunt
- Writers' Café for Teachers
- Science Fairs for Adults
- *Writing Essentials* (Routman, 2005) and *Reading Essentials* (Routman, 2003) Book Talks
- Math Manipulatives for Problem Solving
- The Writing Process
- Behavior Management Strategies

Two formats for the "Mondays at MAE" concept have been quite successful:

1. **Whole Team: Weekly 30-minute team time**

   Create a 30-minute weekly professional development time for whole teams that is not before or after the school day, and does not interfere with teachers' planning time! During the after-school-bus dismissal window, teachers from the various grades walk their students to other grade levels. (The partner classrooms are determined in advance.) Beginning after the first buses are gone reduces the number of students. The teachers who are free of student responsibilities attend Cycle 1 of our "Mondays at MAE" professional development session. The teachers who are watching students attend the presentation the next Monday, during Cycle 2. Each presentation is scheduled twice, once for each cycle.

2. **Vertical Teams: Weekly 30-minute cross-grade-level team time**

   The 30-minute weekly professional development session can be organized for cross-grade-level meetings. During the after-school-bus dismissal window, half the teachers on a team send their students to the classroom of another teacher who is on the same team. This results in half the Data Team at each grade level being free to participate in Cycle 1 of the professional development presentation. Also, this version allows teachers from every grade to participate in professional development *together*. The other half of each grade-level Data Team attends the same presentation during the next week, in Cycle 2.

▪ Specialist-Created Multicultural Lessons: One hour team time

Early dismissals are scheduled several times each year by many school districts. During a few of these early dismissals, our specialists' team provides a one-hour "team lesson" for students focused on multicultural instruction for each grade. Students sing, draw, read, and learn dance steps as our art, music, media, and physical education teachers design lessons to enrich students' knowledge about different cultures. Two early dismissal days are required to complete participation by the whole school. Typically, specialists provide planning time during these early-dismissal days, though it amounts to only 15 minutes. Our teachers agreed to give up their 15 minutes of individual planning time to acquire one hour for their Data Teams to meet on another early dismissal day.

▪ Faculty Team Time: Faculty meetings for Data Teams

Monthly faculty meetings are dedicated to Data Teams. Agenda items are sent by e-mail ahead of time so that faculty meetings can be devoted to action items needed by Data Teams. Specialists and administrators participate during this time to meet with all grade levels.

▪ Front-Loading Data Teams

Monthly, the specialists on the Data Team all go to one grade level for 30 minutes, at student arrival time. This requires a schedule that does not begin specials until 30 minutes into the day. It works best when the team's planning period adjoins this 30 minutes, providing the full 1-1/2 hours for Data Teams.

The methods in these examples still do not provide enough time during the day for Data Teams to accomplish all their responsibilities. Nevertheless, when teachers see that the principal is trying to do everything possible to help them, they appreciate the efforts. Gradually, the conversations that spring from the activities described here expand naturally until these conversations spill out *beyond* the scheduled time.

Time is less of a problem when teachers *believe*. Believe what? When teachers believe that they are doing important work, believe in one another, and believe that every student is capable of excellence, the atmosphere is one of anticipation and eagerness. Throughout the hallways, in lines at the copier, and during lunch, conversations about students' progress continue. Such a deep belief system is what makes Data Teams so effective. As one teacher explained, "We just can't stop talking about this stuff!"

Creative planning for time is necessary to support Data Teams, and concretely demonstrates that school leaders and principals are committed to the Data Team concept. However, the key components for success are the Data Team leaders.

The Role of Data Team Leader

A Data Team leader is required for each and every Data Team. Each leader holds a pivotal position for establishing team trust, support, and reliability. Leaders model a strong work ethic, responsibility, perseverance, enthusiasm for learning, and a strong belief in students, their colleagues, and the process of data-driven decision making (CPA, 2004). When shared with Data Teams, data from individual teachers open the closed doors behind which teachers have traditionally made decisions, in isolation. Student achievement increases, in a natural way, when teachers' personal expectations are examined by colleagues.

Data Team leaders attend a Data Team leader monthly meeting with the principal. One purpose of the monthly meeting is for the principal to provide experiences to develop the Data Team leader's leadership capacity. Knowing that the Data Team leaders are the torchbearers for change and next-step thinking, principals should provide opportunities for Data Team leaders as a group to participate in processes first, ask questions, provide feedback for improvement, and express any resistance or concerns, so that they will be able support the school initiative when it is presented to the faculty. For example, before we introduced the process of collaboratively scoring a common assessment, our Data Team leaders scored assessments together during a Data Team leader meeting with me. This experience informed their discussion about whether the activity was worthwhile and how it affected the teaching–learning process. When the faculty was introduced to this process two weeks later, every Data Team leader was informed and enthusiastic, which made a positive transition much easier and smoother.

Each Data Team Leader comes to the monthly meeting armed with data for discussion about frequent monitoring questions and intervention needs; the whole team of leaders considers these matters with the principal and leadership team. Holistic assessment scores for each teacher on the team are recorded and Compelling Conversations data are compiled in visual data pie charts for each team. All data are distributed to each team leader. The leaders' group also considers potential goals that could be developed by each Data Team during the subsequent Data Team meetings.

Following the monthly meeting with the principal, each Data Team leader schedules a meeting with his or her Data Team and incorporates the leadership skills that were scaffolded during the Data Team leader meeting. Therefore, these meetings provide a safe place where Data Team leaders can experience leadership coaching to enhance their individual team experiences, while maintaining consistency across grade levels.

The Data Team Process

The Data Team works through a five-step, data-driven decision-making process to link data, reflection, and instructional strategies. The teams come together having already had Compelling Conversations with the administrative team. Therefore, team members have already set individual student goals (in Stage 1) for their classes and already have a visual representation (a data pie chart, from Stage 3) of the proficient

Compelling Conversations are a vehicle for integrating reflective practice, data-driven decision making, and instruction toward substantial gains in student achievement.

and nonproficient students. The Data Team process is the opportunity for teachers to widen their scope to their grade level or department. Working collaboratively, they plot grade-level or department data in order to see trends across classrooms, work collectively to brainstorm strategies for improvement, set grade-level or department goals, and determine the next opportunity and metric to assess the selected areas for improvement. Bernhardt explains, "Teams that include processes in their analyses tend to not jump to a solution or conclusions as quickly as those who do not. At some point, when searching for the root cause, one must realize that the problem is really the result. What we are trying to do with these analyses is to uncover why we get our results" (2002, p. 86).

The data-driven decision-making process has been refined to articulate how Data Teams can achieve a specific outcome. The following five steps of the process were designed by The Leadership and Learning Center, formerly Center for Performance Assessment (2006) to guide Data Teams' work:

Step 1: *Collect and chart data.* Student results are categorized by the number and percentage of students performing at proficient or higher levels and the number of nonproficient students in the targeted area of focus.

Step 2: Analyze strengths and obstacles. The proficient students' strengths and nonproficient students' obstacles are determined through reflective inquiry.

Step 3: Establish goals: set, review, and revise. Goals are set, achievement of goals is reviewed, and stated goals are changed if necessary.

Step 4: Select instructional strategies. One or two strategies are chosen by the Data Team to address student obstacles and improve student performance. (These strategies are also modeled to improve consistency of implementation across classrooms.)

Step 5: Determine results indicators. Data Teams determine what evidence will show them that teachers are indeed applying the chosen instructional strategies and that these strategies are in fact helping students to achieve the goals set in step 3.

Step 1: Collect and Chart Data

The Data Team agrees upon the data to be collected about all students from each teacher. Perhaps the team wants to collect data about writing performance, homework completion, or response to literature. The Data Team leader can proceed by asking: "What data would be most beneficial for teachers in order to monitor progress toward end-of-year outcomes/power standards?" (CPA, 2006). The aim is to gather assessment outcomes that provide cause-and-effect feedback to teachers and students, for guiding teaching to improve learning. These outcomes can be drawn from a variety of assessments by a variety of methods, including the formative data transferred from the Compelling Conversations data pie charts.

Transferring Data Pie-Chart Results to Data Teams

The student map completed during Compelling Conversations establishes student goals that were captured in data pie charts, a powerful visual format for sharpening Data Team decisions.

In our particular case, reading comprehension and the skills that improve student performance in that area were the focus. Step 1 of the Data Team process provided a way to analyze our data pie charts collectively. The team analyzes all the team members' data pie charts to determine if any team members need support in helping their students read on or above enrolled grade-level standards. The pie-chart data represent the actual number of students performing at proficient or higher levels and the actual number of students not performing proficiently for each teacher's class.

When this performance information is compared (in step 2 of the Data Team process) to the assessment outcomes entered on the "Collect and Chart Data" form (CPA, 2006), the discrepancies in effect data lead to conversations about students' needs and possible changes in instruction. For example, we determined that some students were receiving reading instruction on grade level, but performed at the nonproficient level on an assessment of written responses to comprehension questions with three or more

Data Team conversations include team questions, such as "These students are not making expected progress, and here are the strategies we've tried. What strategies would be successful?"

details. This conflict in data led to a clearer understanding of students' needs and guided the Data Team goal (step 3 of the Data Team process) for that month. Such understanding is gained when the Data Team selects assessment measures that are tailored to provide specific, targeted information.

A dedicated team leader stopped by before going home for the weekend to say, "I'm going to have a bad weekend. I didn't realize how bad the data would be." This teacher was encouraged by hearing, once again, that data are not good or bad. Data are just information. What you *do* about the data is what matters.

To prepare the data for Data Team meetings, the pie charts for each class are reduced in size so that an entire grade level can fit on *one page* (see Exhibit 2.3A). It is best to share data that are in pie-chart format with teams personally, so as to ameliorate the characteristically cold nature of data with genuine warmth and empathetic concern for teachers.

Compelling Conversations spread the burden of responsibility between the administrative team, teachers, and the visual realm of data pie charts. Friendship-free and emotionally disconnected, data pie charts make the progress of *all* students transparent to Data Teams. Exhibit 2.3B shows very powerfully how many students are achieving Invisible Excellence as well.

Though they are not a complete story, the individual teacher data pie charts do provide consistent achievement "snapshots" of the actual progress that each teacher's class is making *during* the year. Proceed with additional data collection and distribution of data from a holistic perspective.

"We have not been talking about THIS kind of data as teams. Teachers do discuss concerns about one student, but they generally do not put their whole class on the table."

—Jay McTighe

⊚⊚
EXHIBIT 2.3A **Team Pie Charts of Compelling Conversations**

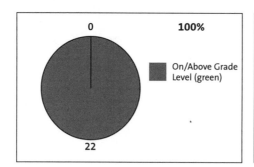

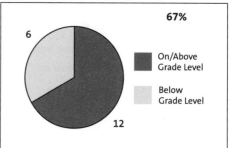

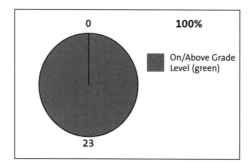

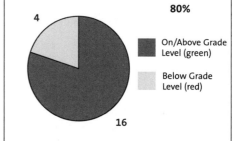

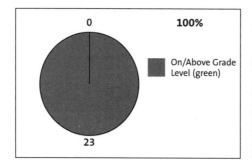

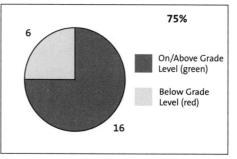

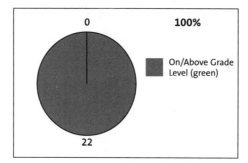

EXHIBIT 2.3B Team Pie Charts of Compelling Conversations

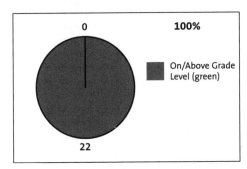

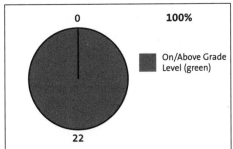

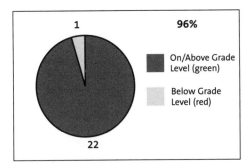

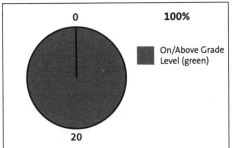

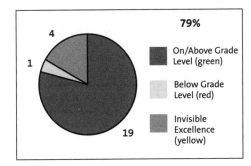

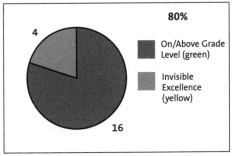

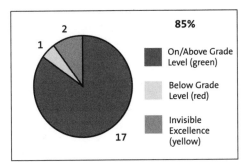

It is tempting for leaders to provide a wealth of data without assuming the concomitant responsibility of providing time and processes for interpreting and using the data. The data-driven decision-making processes (CPA, 2004) provide a clear and consistent method for supporting teams. Stephen Covey aptly noted, "Like it or not, when you pick up one end of the stick, you pick up the other" (2004, p. 48). To get quantitative and qualitative improvement, you must strike a balance between providing additional achievement data and enhancing teacher development and ability regarding data-driven decision making.

The Data Team leader collects the data from each teacher in advance and charts it on the "Collect and Chart Data" Step 1 form (CPA, 2006) (see Exhibit 2.4). Following the collection of data, step 2 of the Data Team process commences with statements and questions about the data.

Step 2: Analyze Strengths and Obstacles

After charting the data, teachers look at the student work they brought with them to the Data Team meeting. Examining these artifacts, they determine students' strengths and weaknesses, and pinpoint consistent and inconsistent skills. These are charted based on the strengths of proficient or higher student performance and obstacles of nonproficient student performance (CPA, 2006) (see Exhibit 2.5). Reflective questions will help determine possible reasons for students not achieving a level of proficiency. The following questions, representing relevance and rigor, may be included:

- Where were the errors? Is there a trend? (CPA, 2006)
- What data tell you that the lessons you are going to teach are the lessons your students need? (CPA, 2006)
- How do these data inform your questions?
- How can this knowledge help influence instructional decisions?
- What questions should be asked about your students?
- Based on current data, how can this Data Team improve its impact on student achievement?

These questions help teachers determine if alignment exists between the levels at which the teacher is delivering instruction to students, assessment outcomes, and students' work samples. The work of identifying obstacles leads to the establishment of one to three specific goals.

◎◎
EXHIBIT 2.4   **Step 1: Collect and Chart Data**

Data Organizer

School _____   Content Areas

Leadership Team _____   _____

Assessment Data _____   _____

_____   _____

_____   Sub-skill Topics

_____   _____

Data Form Completed _____   _____

Content Areas & School Year Data Represent → Enter Grade Level or Special Subgroups ↓	Content _____ School Year _____	Content _____ School Year _____	Content _____ School Year _____	Content _____ School Year _____	Content _____ School Year _____

INSTRUCTIONS: From the data that you have available, complete this chart to get a "snapshot" of student achievement trends and patterns related to your school.

Data-Driven Decision Making
Pages 6–7

EXHIBIT 2.5   **Step 2: Analyze Strenghts and Obstacles**

Examine student work, using a scoring guide or rubric.

Strengths	Obstacles
After examining student work, list strengths of students who were proficient and higher.	List obstacles or reasons why students did not achieve proficiency. Where were there errors? Is there a trend? Are there common errors? What is preventing these students from becoming proficient? Are there misconceptions about concepts or skills?

Adapted from *Data Teams* training manual (2006; The Leadership and Learning Center, formerly Center for Performance Assessment).

Step 3: Establish Goals: Set, Review, Revise

School Improvement Goals

Data Team goal writing begins with the school improvement goals. Our whole school community knows our two goals, one for reading and one for math. When we had more goals, it was like not having any! If students, teachers, staff, and parents do not know the year's goals, what is the point in having them? Mike Schmoker stated, "Many schools tackle only one or two achievement goals annually to prevent the overload that is so clearly the enemy of improvement" (2001, p. 37). Hence, we have only two goals—and both teachers and students know and use them for decisions. With all the assessments that teachers are responsible for, one discussion about goals at the opening of the school year is not sufficient to maintain systems thinking for all decisions. The alignment in Exhibit 2.6 is presented at *every* faculty, team leader, and school improvement meeting to maintain focus.

◎◎
EXHIBIT 2.6   **School Improvement Annual Goals**

School Improvement Annual GOALS for 200___ – 200___

↑ Grade-Level Data Team *Annual* GOAL Statement

↑ Grade-Level Data Team *Monthly* GOAL Statement

↑ Compelling Conversations

    GOALS for individual student performance/assessment

    Whole-class performance outcome

Annual Data Team Goals

Data Teams use current school improvement goals, Data Team information, and the *incoming* Compelling Conversation from June to project their grade's measurable annual team goal (see Exhibit 2.7). Characteristics of Compelling Conversations data that inform measurable annual goals for Data Teams are described in Exhibit 2.8. Although each team sets its own separate *yearly* goal, the guidelines for writing goals are the same for the whole school. Just as we have a process for looking at data, we have a framework for setting goals. Goals must be S-M-A-R-T: Specific, Measurable, Achievable, Relevant, and Timely (CPA, 2006).

◎◎
EXHIBIT 2.7   **School Improvement Annual Goals**

Data Team
Annual GOAL for 200___ – 200___

Improvement Goal Statement:

GOAL: By the end of this year, the percentage of students covered by our Data Team who will be at or above proficiency will increase from _____% at the beginning of 200___ to our GOAL of _____% at the end of 200___, as measured by the _____ formative assessment administered in June 200___.

◎◎
EXHIBIT 2.8   **Informing Measurable Data Team Goals**

Characteristics of Teacher-Generated Student Data from Compelling Conversations

- **Internal**—Compelling Conversations data are generated *directly* from *teachers'* accounts of students' growth. The line of responsibility is pure, direct, and unavoidably honest.

- **Authentic**—Compelling Conversations data are based on teachers' documents, such as grade-level formative assessments and student work.

- **Specifically Accountable**—Compelling Conversations data record the specific *instructional level* on which the teacher is delivering instruction to each student, thus enhancing the capacity to make data-based decisions.

- **Measurable**—The progress that students are making in the classroom is directly measured against the backward-mapped goals established at the beginning of the year. Compelling Conversations investigate and compare students' progress toward grade-level standards, thus reversing the bell-curve expectation that some students must fail.

- **Current**—Compelling Conversations data are job-embedded. Therefore, these data are used to make immediate instructional modifications.

- **Responsible**—The rubber hits the road right here. It cannot be said that Compelling Conversations data are a one-time snapshot, meaningless because of being standardized or lacking connections with the curriculum; this assessment of performance represents each teacher's instructional decisions, about every child, *during* the school year.

- **Respected**—Decisions are *valued* by colleagues because *every* teacher in the school knows and understands that the standards integrated at each grade level are consistent.

The process for setting SMART goals has five components: (1) specifically targeting a subject area, grade level, or student population; and requiring that the goals be (2) measurable, (3) achievable in percentage gains or increases, (4) relevant to standards and urgently needed, and (5) timely, so that ongoing monitoring ensures that midcourse corrections will be made as needed, and also ensures consistency in expectations. A Data Team's annual goal should exceed the previous grade's end-of-year achievement results. This is the opposite of comparing one grade level to itself. Instead, SMART goals focus on students in each grade as they progress through school.

Monthly Data Team Goals

Monthly Data Team goals (see Exhibit 2.9) are written to establish an achievement focus for continuous evaluation of students' progress. The monthly Data Team

EXHIBIT 2.9   Step 3: Establish Goals: Set, Review, Revise

Start with the data from the pre-assessment that were recorded in step 1. Establish the growth target as the expected percent, or actual number, of students proficient and higher at the end of the instructional time.

SMART Goal Statement:

The percentage or number of [student group] scoring proficient and higher in [content area] will increase from [current percentage/number] to [goal percentage/number] by the end of [month or quarter] as measured by [assessment tool] administered on [specific date].

Example: Percentage of Grade 5 students scoring proficient and higher in math problem solving will increase from 43% to 58% by October 30 (in 4 weeks) as measured by a teacher-created math assessment administered on October 30.

GOAL: The percentage of _____ scoring proficient and higher in _____ will increase from _____% to _____% by the end of _____ as measured by _____ administered on _____.

GOAL: The number of _____ scoring proficient and higher in _____ will increase from _____ to _____ by the end of _____ as measured by _____ administered on _____.

Adapted from *Data Teams* training manual (2006; The Leadership and Learning Center, formerly Center for Performance Assessment).

goals support the team's annual goal, thereby maintaining alignment between Data Teams' work and the school improvement goals. A crucial component of goal setting is increasing student success through teacher monitoring of students' progress.

The monthly team goals reflect the needs of all the students, as indicated by data. Marzano explains, "Two key elements are required to implement challenging goals and effective feedback: first, challenging goals must be established for all students; second, effective feedback must be specific and formative" (2003, p. 46). The Data Team continues to assess students throughout the month, using the "Data Team Time 'On the Clock'" suggestions in this chapter, and to provide

As a team leader explained, "We bring three samples of work to our Data Team meetings: a sample of work before the goal was established, a sample from the middle of the month, and a sample from the end of the month!"

the Data Team leader with the resulting assessment data, which will be analyzed with the team and principal at their monthly meeting.

To continuously build leadership capacity within a faculty, compile all the Data Teams' monthly team goals and share them during monthly faculty meetings. The purposes of sharing each grade's monthly goal with the whole school include:

1. Increasing communication about grade-level standards *across* grade levels

2. Demonstrating that monthly Data Team goals are so important that the principal and school leaders read and integrate them into a whole-school goal review

3. Continuing to expand teachers' capacity for setting goals through sharing models of measurable goals that were written by their colleagues

4. Raising the bar between grade levels so that "silos" of excellence in one grade level become shared excellence for all

Sharing monthly goal statements provides a backdrop for whole-school awareness of each team's level of progress.

The first time I shared the concept of having our teams write annual and monthly team goals (because goals increase both student achievement and communication), I could immediately see consternation in the teachers' faces. Two teachers expressed their concern: "This will be one more thing to do." I assured them that it was! However, I also created time during the school day, on the clock and not during their planning time, for teams to write goals (see the "Data Team Time 'On the Clock'" section in this chapter). Do teams ever receive enough time? No. Nevertheless, when teachers see that the principals are doing their utmost to generate more time for them, and they *know* the administration honestly believes in them, positive attitudes prevail.

The results from implementation of the goals inform the teachers on the team about the next instructional decisions they need to make. The results guide teachers and students toward the next teaching point, or reveal the need to revisit a previous instructional goal that was not achieved. Annual and monthly Data Team goals that support the school improvement goals help to obtain desired achievement results for students because "goals and the commitment they generate are the glue that holds teams together" (Schmoker, 1999, p. 24).

Step 4: Select Instructional Strategies

The Data Team uses the "Select Instructional Strategy" chart (CPA, 2006) (see Exhibit 2.10) to collaborate on one or two strategies they all agree to implement

⊚⊚
EXHIBIT 2.10 **Step 4: Select Instructional Strategies**

- Which strategies will have the greatest impact on student learning?
- What strategies are other teachers implementing with a high degree of success? Should these practices be replicated?
- Focus on strategies that are either within your direct control or your direct influence.

Effective Teaching Strategies	Learning Environment	Materials for Teachers and for Students	Time—Duration of the Specific Teaching of Concepts and Skills	Assessments, Assignments
____ Comparison ____ Classification ____ Metaphor ____ Analogy				
____ Summarization ____ Note Taking				
____ Effort* ____ Recognition*				
____ Homework* ____ Practice*				
____ Nonlinguistic Representations				
____ Cooperative Learning				
____ Establishment of Objectives* ____ Feedback*				
____ Hypothesis Generation ____ Hypothesis Testing				
____ Cues ____ Questions ____ Advance Organizers				
____ Nonfiction Writing				

* = strategies recommended for daily use

Adapted from *Data Teams* training manual (2006; The Leadership and Learning Center, formerly Center for Performance Assessment).

based on the expected impact on student learning. The strategies will support the monthly goal. Strategies can be expanded for teams when the principal supports allocation of financial resources for instructional materials and additional time for collaboration and peer visitations.

Step 5: Determine Results Indicators

The results will reveal the effectiveness of the strategy; that is, its capacity to achieve the goal determined in step 3. The specific results indicators depicting what your team expects to see are recorded on the step 5 form, Determine Results Indicators (CPA, 2006) (see Exhibit 2.11). The five steps of the Data Team process incorporate three critical levels of information that support accountability.

Three Levels of Accountability

Embedded in the Data Teams process are three tiers of accountability (Reeves, 2004).

- ▪▪ Tier 1 accountability indicators include test scores and external outcome indicators. Such test scores do not lead to understanding of students' needs.

EXHIBIT 2.11   **Step 5:   Determine Results Indicators**

Results indicators complete the statement: "When this strategy is implemented, we expect to see the following evidence...."

- ▪ Describe the explicit behaviors (both student and adult behaviors) you EXPECT to see as a result of implementing the strategies identified in step 4.

- ▪ How will you know that the strategies are working? What evidence or learning behaviors do you expect to see in students as a result of the instruction? What are proficient students able to do successfully?

- ▪ Which strategies are working for most students? What must be done in addition with certain students?

1.

2.

3.

4.

Adapted from *Data Teams* training manual (2006; The Leadership and Learning Center, formerly Center for Performance Assessment).

■■ Tier 2 indicators are measurable internal indicators of professional practices that reflect how adults influence students' achievement. The results from Compelling Conversations with each teacher about every child's current performance, as opposed to test scores, reside at Tier 2. The results depict progress by every student, the whole class, the whole grade, and the whole school during the year, thus providing critical accountability information for Data Teams.

■■ The Tier 3 indicator is a school narrative providing a qualitative context for Tier 1 data. While presenting at the Principal's Academy at Harvard University, Douglas Reeves asked, "What is the story behind the numbers?" This question lingered in my mind because writing a Tier 3 narrative helps you to *know more than you know you know.*

Writing Narratives: Team and School

The team narrative (Exhibit 2.12) supports teams during the challenging task of integrating multiple sources of incoming data during step 1 of the Data Team process and generating monthly goals during step 3. The written team narrative, in which Data Teams synthesize their rationale into a paragraph, incorporates the writing process for goal setting. The process of writing adds a powerful level of clarity to the process. The following team narrative regarding monthly team goals is from a first-grade team.

🎯 ZOOMING IN ON SUCCESS

Our holistic scores did not achieve our goal in reading on this assessment. Probable causes are:

1. Students read test independently with no teacher support
2. There was minimal picture support
3. Students were not familiar with poetry format
4. Students had to utilize the higher-level thinking skills of interpretation and inference

After discussing the possible causes for the decline in reading scores, we will continue to provide independent reading time. We will provide instruction on interpretation and inference. We will determine whether the students who scored low were below-level readers. If so, on our next assessment, those students reading below grade level will have the test read to them to provide us with a measure of their comprehension ability. The on- and above-grade-level readers will continue to take their assessments independently and they will be scored with a rubric. We will continue to monitor our Conversations data outcomes for evidence of whole-grade progress.

The team leader, Kay Hayes, explained, "A team needs a purpose, a goal. That's how conversations about teamwork begin. We become invested in it together. Until we established monthly goals, it was difficult to meet about student progress because some teachers would ask, "What do you want us to do?" Now the team asks, "What do we want our students to accomplish?"

EXHIBIT 2.12 **Monthly Team Narrative**

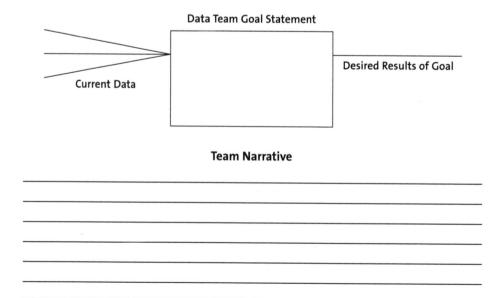

Monthly Team Narrative
What is the story behind the numbers?

School assessment scores are not the end result of instruction; rather, they are information for improving students' learning.

Consider the factors that affect your monthly Data Team goal for students' progress in this organizer, then describe your goal in a team narrative.

Data Team Goal Statement

Desired Results of Goal

Current Data

Team Narrative

Team narratives are another opportunity to increase vertical team communication. When teachers are expected to write team narratives, a layer of communication at the Data Team level is added. To ease this initiative into your school, consider summarizing monthly goals from all grades and then write a "School Narrative" summary for the faculty meeting.

The following is an example of a school narrative that was gleaned from the team narratives for March:

> Our school's Data Team goals for March were based on evidence from a variety of job-embedded data and formal data. Holistic assessments, state assessments, and Compelling Conversations data assisted in decision making. In addition, informal assessments, such as student conversations, class work, oral responses, cold text practice, weekly story assessments, and discrepancies between selected response assessments and transferring understanding into written responses, were used to establish the team goals. The Data Team goals for March, throughout our grades, focused on the desired results for student improvement in fluency, inferencing, and oral and written responses.
>
> Faculty meetings should be devoted to Data Teams because time is vital and it demonstrates that the principal regards time for Data Teams as a high priority. It also provides collaboration time for holding Science Fairs for Adults. During the Science Fair, each Data Team creates and displays on a trifold display board, items from the three tiers of accountability (Reeves, 2004), with the team narrative on the right side of the display.
>
> *When our team met in the past, you would hear, "This is how you do this."*
>
> *Now you hear, "How can we solve this problem?"*

How Will the Story End?

While asking, "What is the story behind the numbers?," our assistant principal, Sheri Maring, continued reflecting by asking teachers, "How will the story end?"

Conversations with every teacher about the progress of each of their students focuses attention on the importance of teachers' decisions. The matrix called "What Is the Story Behind the Numbers?" (see Exhibit 2.13) charts each student's relevant outcomes in several columns by the teacher's name. This matrix can be used in high schools, middle schools, and content areas, as well as elementary grades. These charts help Data Teams connect relevant internal Tier 2 data with external Tier 1 scores by creating a context for whole-team reflective inquiry. Some

◎◎
EXHIBIT 2.13 **Matrix for Telling the "Story Behind the Numbers"**

WHAT IS THE STORY BEHIND THE NUMBERS?

Analyzing Your Team's Data

Focus on <u>EVERY</u> student's relevant __[READING]__ outcomes

Teachers on Team	1. Students not yet making at least one year's growth (AYP)	2. Students scoring below proficient on state reading assessment	3. Students considered for retention last year	4. Students needing to maintain Invisible Excellence	5. Students needing to achieve Invisible Excellence this year
1.					
2.					
3.					
4.					

questions generated by Data Teams when entering the student names in this chart were as follows:

- There is an increase in the number of students entering our school for whom we have no data at all. How can we determine the most appropriate instruction for them?

- Why are students who were considered for retention not retained? What were the reasons that they were considered for retention?

- I don't want a child to fly under the radar. I don't want someone to ask, "What happened to this child?" So, what else can we consider now?

- How can we improve content literacy (especially in high school)?

How will this story end? Each child will be in the hands of the Data Team of teachers. With Data Teams and the reliable data they generate, everyone knows the intended endings. Samples include:

- "These four students, who achieved Invisible Excellence by achieving more than one year's progress last year (see Chapter 3), scored proficient on the state assessment!"

- "These two students, who made Invisible Excellence last year, are now reading successfully on grade level."

These student success stories stem from capacity, both leadership and team, that began with Compelling Conversations and were developed further through Data Team processes.

Building Team Capacity

Sharing formative data shifts communication patterns between teachers, within teams, and throughout schools. Data Teams of teachers, who regularly discuss success stories about midcourse corrections (Reeves, 2004), establish new standards of collegiality, as described by an excellent teacher and Data Team leader, Janet Stevens.

ZOOMING IN ON SUCCESS

I have a few students making about 1½ years' growth this year. They will not be on grade level this year, but in two years, they should be on level! I had conversations with our specialists about ideas for additional support. Our conversations resulted in more instructional time for students.

We scheduled one extra 40-minute reading class every Friday afternoon at 2:20. Jenny, our reading specialist, and Hope, our special education teacher, come too. As a team, we instruct these students one more time on the skills and strategies that were taught during that week. This class session seems to "set" the skills so these students can remember them and use them with understanding.

This conversation sounds natural. *It is not.* It springs from a learned and practiced process. The Data Team process and structures within data-driven decision making support team conversations about students. Commitment of time to meet as a team is stronger when meetings are structured around high expectations, setting goals, improving student achievement, helping colleagues sort through complexities related to specific students, and sharing success strategies as Janet did.

As student achievement improves, teachers acquire confidence in how well they know their learners and in their instructional decision making. Maintaining this level of commitment requires strong leadership at the Data Team level. The wonderfully positive Data Team cycle infuses the culture with a strong belief system that even reaches students' beliefs and self-confidence about their own potential.

Summary

Chapter 2 described the conditions for success that Douglas Reeves (2004) and Mike Schmoker (2001) have identified as crucial for schools desiring improvement. Included in the structures are data-driven decision-making concepts (CPA, 2004) and the five-step process for Data Teams (CPA, 2006). Compelling Conversations data are incorporated to guide individual teachers and students in achieving goals, while supporting the establishment of goals for and by Data Teams.

CHAPTER 3

CONVERSATIONS: *A Collaborative Model for Instruction*

Essential Question: *How can the themes revealed in Compelling Conversations and the data patterns that emerge redefine beliefs, roles, and instructional models?*

Chapter Foreword   BETSY CUNNINGHAM

"Traditionally, students were put in reading groups and expected to make this current year's growth. There was no stress on last year's growth also. Without Conversations, gaps are created. If we did not have Conversations with the Student Map, it would be impossible to realize at the beginning of school that students made this much progress last year." Thus Betsy Cunningham, a classroom teacher, conveys the potential of Compelling Conversations for transferring learning between grade levels. Conversations also address the need for ownership of reading strategies and skills to be transferred directly to students.

Introduction

Traditional models and traditional perceptions get in the way of seeing things differently. Through Compelling Conversations, it is possible to learn what belief systems are currently operating and what data exist (or do not exist) to support those beliefs. Our discoveries made during Compelling Conversations changed beliefs about achievement for particular student groups, the way colleagues worked together, and the structured reading programs. For example, at our school, we were able to establish a new belief system congruent with our mission statement. The difference was that we were dead serious about this mission: *success with a joy for learning and pride in a caring community.*

Thankfully, enough trust had been established for teachers such as Hope Sachwald and Ned Landis, our speech and language and special education teachers, to disclose their perceptions so that we could begin constructing a new reality. Like scientists, we just need to create the right conditions to encourage growth. It becomes a joint quest to create models that change the trajectory of learning for all students, especially special education students, and to monitor their progress. In addition to increasing expectations and developing action plans for instruction and future monitoring, conversations help redefine the relationships and roles of administrators, specialists, and classroom teachers. As resource teachers begin collaborating to craft a new vision and new methods for applying collective expertise, more teachers begin thinking flexibly about all resources. Conversations became an integral aspect of the culture, leading to the instructional delivery models crafted by Sheri Maring, our assistant principal, and Jenny Barnes, our reading specialist.

> *"This is a powerful change of roles and a cultural shift."*
>
> —Jay McTighe, 2005

Finding Students Before We Lose Them

Three purposes align needs of individual students with the best instructional and human resources to help those students become successful learners. Compelling Conversations invite us to:

- Continuously identify and respond to the instructional needs of all learners
- Increase expectations for all students, including identified subgroups
- Revisit school standards to ensure that all students, including those who are on and above grade level, are attaining their potential

Compelling Conversations dedicate time to uncovering emerging kernels of concern about specific students *before* those students develop serious and complex learning problems. Some readers, for example, are reading successfully but without confidence. Their success is *vulnerable:* one extended illness (with the concomitant time out of school) could wreck their frail understanding of the reading process. These children frequently go unnoticed. Students who are vulnerable learners wander somewhere in between needing teacher scaffolding for optimal learning and just wanting to be acknowledged by teacher affirmations. These students can be found in the classroom landscape between the steady, secure readers and those who require formal intervention plans. Jenny Barnes shared the following exchange with me, in which one of the keys to unlocking this child's potential was revealed.

 ZOOMING IN ON SUCCESS

"Janelle, I'm worried about you. You've missed eight words on the page already."

"Is eight too many?"

"Yes."

"Would you like it if I only miss two or three?"

"Yes!"

So, that's what Janelle started to do!

A conversation in which the teacher let Janelle "know where she stood" as a reader was the motivation for this child. Through this interaction, the teacher learned not to assume that the child knew or understood the expectations. The teacher had to explicitly communicate the standards for learning. Within one marking period, Janelle was reading on her enrolled grade level! Janelle's teacher had backward-mapped goals during our Compelling Conversation, and the chosen strategies included plans for double-instructed reading. Janelle did not go unnoticed.

As one classroom teacher explained, "I felt that conversations were beneficial because they kept me on track! I had a clear idea of where my struggling students needed to be at various points in the year. If they were not approaching their goals, I knew I had to reevaluate my instructional strategies and try something else."

During Compelling Conversations, we talk about students, such as Janelle, who are struggling. These students are not special education students. Students who are *not* formally identified to receive additional services, such as special education support, may still display a need for more intensive instruction. Increased intensity, using specific, research-based instructional strategies, fills in the gaps that some students develop. Comprehension may be viewed as "the essence of reading" (Durkin, 1993). Under this definition, cognitive strategies that support comprehension improvement include: reciprocal teaching processes of prediction, student questioning, clarification, and summarization (Palinscar & Brown, 1984); metacognitive monitoring of text (Piercy, 2000); vocabulary preteaching (Wixson, 1986); and fluency guidance during oral reading (Strecker, Roser, & Martinez, 1998).

In addition, meeting some students' needs requires a combination of behavioral, emotional, and social support, all of which is focused on during Compelling Conversations. Exhibit 3.1 lists examples of student behaviors and areas of concerns that have been discussed during conversations and indicate that instructional modifications should be considered.

Surfacing Our Beliefs and Expectations

Our core *belief* is simple: students who leave elementary or middle school reading and performing math successfully on their enrolled grade level have a better chance. They just do. In their middle and high school years, students who are not

---

EXHIBIT 3.1   **Student Behaviors Displayed by Some Struggling Learners**

NOTE: These students do not receive special education support.

- Classwork, report-card grades, and state assessment results are significantly discrepant
- Displays much anxiety when faced with challenging activities
- Cannot demonstrate comprehension on written tasks
- Needs much additional time for learning strategies and comprehending
- Written responses do not reflect the student's oral comprehension
- Vocabulary retention and transfer into writing are below proficient
- Very motivated, but does not transfer skills and strategies
- Difficulty with writing and explaining thinking
- Chews on clothing or hair while writing

successful frequently deal with self-esteem issues. These problems can spill over into their choices about peer groups and how to spend their free time; this is often when drug and alcohol use gain fateful holds on young lives. Fighting for kids is what we're about, as indicated in our vision/mission: "*Success* with a *joy* for learning and pride in a *caring* community." Caring about kids' future lives is a part of the big picture of developing learning success for them. Sending a higher percentage of kids with high scores to middle school does *not* stir excitement deep within our hearts! When the administrative team and teachers passionately strive for each student to be successful as an individual, caring is ignited and passion guides decisions. An entire school file of test scores, with elaborate spreadsheets devoid of personal meaning, can never incite the passion for teaching and learning the way each one of our student's lives grabs our heartstrings. Kay Hayes, who was a first-grade teacher before becoming an assistant principal, explains, "School success begins with the principal talking, reflecting, and expecting high standards by making conversations a priority."

Leading Toward a Culture of Beliefs

The principal has the capacity to communicate and interconnect with all classroom teachers, school resource teachers, and central office resource personnel, and to seek financial support on behalf of teachers and their students. Conversations between the administrative team and each teacher are the golden key to the passion that constitutes the soul of the culture. Our Compelling Conversations create time to communicate a shift in the core belief system—from delivering instruction to developing learning—so that the whole child's life benefits, not just the student we see from 8:00 A.M. to 3:00 P.M.

Redefining Beliefs

A new era is here: it is time for principals and school leaders to inhabit this present reality with honesty. It is just *wrong* to continue to lead schools, filled with hundreds of young lives, needing timeless skills so they can courageously face unimaginable futures, by following the traditional leadership model equipped with the usual end-of-year state assessment scores. These structures were only minimally successfully two decades ago. Today? Tapping into the higher needs of teachers, Compelling

What will your teachers say about student-centered accountability? Teachers are relieved to know that their hard work is respected. Their students' progress is not discounted because of poorly founded assumptions that knowledge dissolves during summer vacation.

Conversations become the voice of the culture—a voice of believing. "Voice is revealed as we face our greatest challenges and … makes us equal to them" (Covey, 2004, p. 5).

As school leaders' and teachers' beliefs in one another increase, beliefs in children also intensify. "Learning magic begins only when children believe they can succeed" (Routman, 2003, p. 9). A visitor to our school quoted a comment one of our teachers made: "Sometimes I think my principal believes in me more than I believe in myself." When teachers feel this belief, they can become it. A strong cultural voice transfers into *believing* in students. "When you engage in work that taps your talent and fuels your passion—that rises out of a great need in the world that you feel drawn by conscience to meet—therein lies your voice, your calling, your soul's code" (Covey, 2004, p. 5).

 ## ZOOMING IN ON SUCCESS

Betsy Cunningham explains her beliefs to her students. "I tell them at the beginning of second grade that they can be reading successfully this year. I tell them where they are (data based on formative assessments), and where they need to be. I show it to them visually. I tell them that they are going to. They don't really have a choice!"

Betsy's message to each student is: "I believe you will read successfully! I know you can."

Believing in All Students

One purpose of Compelling Conversations is to increase expectations of all students, including our special needs population. "You teach special needs students the way you teach all students. You hold *high* expectations for each one of them" (Routman, 2003, p. 8).

The closing of the legendary "achievement gap" for special education students did not occur by focusing on increasing our school's slope on the state achievement tests. It was not the result of additional state funds. When Compelling Conversations shift concentration from state assessment outcomes *to the slope of each individual student*, state assessment scores increase. However, we did not begin with those results. What we discovered about the connections between beliefs and instruction, during our conversations, propelled us toward a new definition of our roles and instructional models.

Redefining Roles

Is only one child at a time enough? It is for that child. That child may be a middle school adolescent who now believes in himself or herself enough to make good choices. Compelling Conversations are a commitment of ourselves—one person, one voice—to make schools better for all. Sometimes our conversations are about "impossible" goals, especially for our special education students.

 ZOOMING IN ON SUCCESS

Late one afternoon, Hope Sachwald stopped by. Because she is one of the finest teachers of special education students anywhere, our staff has enormous respect for Hope's thoughts. That afternoon, Hope had determined that it was time somebody on the staff told me the truth: "Thommie, you just don't understand. All students cannot be expected to achieve the same standards." That led to a breakthrough conversation. I asked Hope how everyone could be so certain of this, if we have never had high expectations for all students. By the end of this conversation, Hope said she would think things over.

Gradually, Hope and her entire special education department were providing instruction to meet the IEP goals by blending special education instruction with the classroom teacher's instruction. Although our special education teachers had been using a classroom inclusion model to "push in" required IEP services, the instruction was different from the classroom teacher's lesson outcomes. Now, instruction is connected, as depicted in Exhibit 3.2. Hope's changed belief structure directly affected the models of instruction used throughout our school.

Today, Hope reflects with colleagues, "We used to teach with the model: 'This is *yours* to teach and this is *mine*.' It was undifferentiated special education instruction. Language–you, Writing–me. Why are these separate? It doesn't matter who provides the service!" Her sentiments were echoed by another colleague: "Our

EXHIBIT 3.2   **Connected Instruction Model**

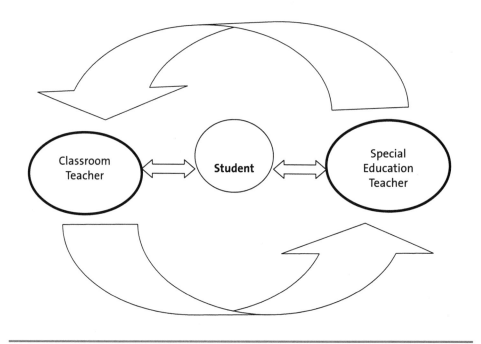

Compelling Conversations gave me multiple opportunities to collaborate with professionals on new methods for an overall increase in academic achievement for those struggling students." The Put Reading First Initiative (CIERA, 2001) supports this viewpoint and approach by explaining that all children, even those who are widely discrepant, benefit from opportunities to participate in an inclusive classroom environment, thus gaining access to vocabulary and comprehension strategies taught during mainstream instruction. Teachers should include all children, even those requiring additional support, within the entire session of classroom instruction to reduce fragmentation of the special needs students' instructional program.

Hope continues, "Now, both the classroom teacher and I teach the students what they need to be successful as readers. We look at what the child needs and determine who can best provide it." Simultaneously, this acts as job-embedded, one-on-one staff development, because excellent instruction is being modeled by our resource teachers for new classroom teachers—without having to tell new staff that *this* is how you should be teaching. This professional development is vital in schools that are experiencing significant change, such as ours, in which the demands of increased enrollment mean that one-third of our staff is nontenured.

When conversations are based on beliefs and supported with data, students' lives change.

Today's diversity of students is too great for the classroom teacher to be able to meet all the needs of all students. Many students require "*three or four times as much instruction* as the average student if they are to maintain normal progress in reading." Nevertheless, not having enough time can no longer be an excuse for lack of student progress. Our children's futures depend on the principal's commitment to *find* instructional time. "Schools with the largest gains made dramatic changes in their schedules. At the elementary level, they routinely devoted three hours each day to literacy, with two hours of reading and one hour of writing" (Reeves, 2004, p. 68). What is needed is *coordinated instruction* between the classroom teacher, special education teachers, and reading specialists. "Educators must tell their story, including the extraordinary efforts they make on behalf of students and parents every day. This will require a combination of quantitative measurement of their daily activities and a qualitative description of their intensity, intellect, and commitment" (Reeves, 2004, p. 15). The administrator in the building is the crux of this coordination.

The Principal

The reason the principal is central to change is that the role of the principal allows access to unique resources. If taken for granted, though, these can be underestimated or overlooked altogether. Also, the entire administrative team, including the assistant principal, school counselor, student services team, and all curriculum and assessment supervisors, possesses a wealth of resources. Some of the free, powerful resources that can be utilized to support communication in a collaborative culture include:

- Confidentiality—increases trust
- Commitment—generates commitment from the entire staff
- Fairness—leads to acceptance as standards are raised
- Empathy about teachers' frustrations—extends trust
- Expanded teachers' skills—increase knowledge about research and allow instructional decisions to be made based on research regarding connections between data, standards, and knowledge of the child
- Monitoring opportunities—enhance ability to gauge the progress of each student toward his or her goals, then guide modification of instructional decisions

▪ Decisions—based on reason and data

▪ Commitment—to excellence

▪ Knowledge—of whole-school resources that are accessible through the office of the principal

A clear line of sight and firm connection between responsibilities of the administrative team (as a whole) and teachers is needed for today's children to successfully grow into their lives. Sharing these resources while collaborating about the needs of students helps to strengthen the bond between the principal and teachers.

Coordinated Instruction

During Compelling Conversations, as the administrative team integrates all available resources to help individual teachers with their students, the roles of administrators and teachers fuse, creating a unique connectivity that overcomes the fragmentation inherent in the usual organizational structure. This is in sharp contrast to the traditional delineation and strict separation of roles. Classroom teachers, reading teachers, special education teachers, speech and language teachers, specialist teams, health teachers, and administrative teams: we all need to explore ways to increase collaborative efforts to benefit our students. Our division of roles, expectations, and responsibilities for student learning feeds the fragmentation, which is one of the main problems with education (Fullen, 2001, p. 108).

In contrast, Compelling Conversations offer time to blur the lines between roles and to be heard. Meeting students' unique needs requires exactly what teachers have requested for generations: more *time for teaching* and *smaller class sizes.* Yes, their honest requests are challenging to school budgets. After years of going through separate State Department of Education and district programs, though, at-risk students are still making only minimal progress, despite the millions of dollars spent on the newest assessments and the buzziest programs. *Isn't it time to listen to our teachers?*

Kids need more time. How do you find them more time? With a DIR tutor, an older student reading to them, or sometimes just by increasing communication with the student's home, time for learning increases.

During Compelling Conversations with teachers, I have heard teachers say, "Roberto is making progress, and he could be reading successfully on grade-level standards—if I had some additional time with *just him.*" Regie Routman explains that disadvantaged students do not need different instruction, they need the same excellent instruction that is provided to all students. "Disadvantaged students just need more of it" (2005, p. 56). Increased time for instruction is a priority of administrators that has immediate impact on student achievement.

Teachers see clearly what is needed: "After our reading group, Dillon, Tracie, and Dion need time to practice the skills I've been teaching, like summarization, while they are reading. They will need to use this skill while they are reading independently if they are to become successful readers." Even as teachers voice frustration with increasing expectations, and request more time to provide instruction connected to the grade-level curriculum, they get the new packaged programs designed for separate instruction that are delivered to schools.

What's a principal to do?

What would *you* do?

Redefining Models of Instruction

The only honest choice is to support our shared belief that we have to give kids a better chance. I knew I had to find ways to give teachers (and students) more teaching time, in smaller groups, to provide good, solid instruction. Such a fundamental decision redefined several models of instruction, moving away from the fragmented delivery of "instructional services" toward teaching students as individual learners. This decision made teaching that was devoid of isolated programs appear to be just the latest innovation, though, so we had to fight hard to prove its worth.

To support teachers' voices, we wrote waivers requesting that we *not* participate in remedial programs that required isolated instruction out of a box. Why? In addition to the facts that these programs do not know our students' needs or our teachers' strengths, when students fail, it is easy to blame "the box." Teachers from other schools would say, "Of course the students did poorly. I could have told you that it was not an effective program." How does a principal hold a box accountable? Besides, Mr. Scott Foresman's signature does not appear on every report card each year.

If students demonstrate progress on standardized assessments, waivers can be requested for another year. If a purchased program does *not* demonstrate success in one year, is it removed? You already know the answer.

My experience leads me to agree with the eloquent and passionate words of my colleague Regie Routman: "We need to be vigilant about new programs and materials that districts are thinking about adopting. At best, any program, no matter how good it is, is a resource and tool. It can never take the place of the knowledgeable teacher. Increasingly, restrictive programs and materials are becoming part of our classrooms without our input or approval. The voices wanting to 'fix' education are loud and insistent, but they are not the teachers' voices" (Routman, 2003, p. 200). She continues by explaining, "Students in classrooms with effective teachers are better readers regardless of the approach, program, or materials the teachers use" (Routman, 2003, p. 191).

Imagine! Replacing prepackaged intervention programs and fragmented skills with commonsense, solid, sound instruction. However, in addition to reducing the numbers and layers of separate programs, the needs for *time* and reduced *class size* had to be addressed if we were to respond to the student-specific, accurate, and timely achievement data generated by the well-founded and well-researched practice of frequent monitoring by Data Teams.

The accurate data being provided to teachers from formative assessments usually results in an increase in the numbers of students requiring additional instructional support. Some students require more instructional time to achieve success with grade-level expectations. These groups of children requiring additional support are not, however, separated from the classroom teacher. They receive resource support in the form of double-instructed reading (DIR).

Achievement with Double-Instructed Reading

For a leader, knowing the barriers to student achievement is half the battle. Still, once that information is available, it must be acted upon. Support is provided by each state's Response to Intervention Framework. At http://state.rti4success.org/, there is a link to each state's Response to Intervention (RTI) document. For example, Maryland's framework document defines RTI as being "a systematic school-wide multi-tiered approach that when implemented with fidelity fosters prevention of achievement and behavioral difficulties while providing intervention at increasing levels of intensity matched to the academic and behavioral needs of students," (MSDE, p. 2).

Consistency and clarity are vital components of a plan that provides the opportunity for all students to reach their potential. An excellent resource from The Leadership and Learning Center is the Power Strategies for Response to Intervention Seminar, which provides in-depth information and clarity about the Response to Intervention process to support tiered interventions. The three tiers of intervention described in this seminar provide descriptions of a rich variety of Tier I and Tier II interventions, including instructional activities that can be readily integrated during classroom instruction. The collaborative process of effectively selecting aligned interventions can enhance a school system's ability to overcome identified barriers to student achievement.

One example of a Tier II intervention that provides success for students is double-instructed reading. It provides students and teachers with much-needed additional support that is grounded in conditional knowledge research (Paris, Wixson, & Palinscar, 1986).

The Need for Double-Instructed Reading

Try asking the staff of a school, "Why are students not achieving success on state assessments?" The paper will fly off the chart stand with all the reasons, most of which are outside the teachers' control. What are the factors that limit students' growth at your school? Determining the response to that question is one of the greatest leadership challenges facing principals, especially new principals. Not only are there multiple causes, some causes are indiscernible. Everything feels out of our control. If the barriers to student success were readily apparent, our teachers' jobs would be easy. Also, I, as the principal, would be dancing the Six Flags Amusement Park jig down the school hallways, because every student would be successful.

Alas, reality begs to differ. Still, a school can bite pieces off this huge, seemingly indigestible chunk. For one, real barriers are indicated by state reading assessments throughout the country. For example, when I became principal, only 39 percent of third-graders were achieving "satisfactory" levels on the state assessment. Nevertheless, just as water-stained ceiling tiles are not the cause of a leaky roof; poor performance on assessments is not the reason kids cannot read well—it's a symptom, not a cause. So, what are the reasons?

The easiest place to start is with what you know. Acknowledging that *"We're losing our kids and no one understands why"* (see Chapter 1) was an honest first step. Recognizing that communication was the root cause of our ignorance helped us begin to build understanding. Compelling Conversations help leaders incorporate leadership strategies as the next steps for improving learning. Backward-mapping goals for each student (see Chapter 1), monitoring progress with teachers regularly (see Chapter 1), and creating time for Data Teams to establish goals based on their data (see Chapter 2) are three leadership strategies incorporated within Compelling Conversations.

The "losing our kids" aspect of what we know as leaders deserves much attention. Conversations conveyed, in general, that teachers believed that *time* for additional instruction and *smaller class sizes* were two factors that would help more students learn successfully. Then the teachers' barriers were in my lap. Can a principal find more *time* to teach kids? Can a principal make *class sizes smaller*?

Does a principal have control over the district-determined class size? Can a principal demand that the superintendent assign more teachers to a school? What if your school is not a Title I school? Imagine having low scores but no additional federal funds. *Would more money do any good?* Douglas Reeves (2005) reminds us that low scores are low scores! With life being multivariant, the correlation of low achievement with children living in poverty, or having/needing special education services, does *not* establish causation of low scores. My school's low scores were not any better than Baltimore City's low scores. We can no longer exempt special needs children from achieving standards, nor should we expect less for them because of terrible life situations. If schools do not receive extra funding, what is a principal to do?

Research Base for Double-Instructed Reading

In an attempt to uncover barriers to our students' achievement, I returned to the research about reading while also revisiting our school's data. My goal was to understand how to improve communication while addressing teachers' continuing concerns about time and class size. I turned to the classic research about how knowledge is actually learned, in order to structure a program that would meet the needs of our struggling population.

I found that cognitive and developmental psychologists have examined the kinds of knowledge that are acquired as learners change from novice readers to expert readers. The experts emphasized *declarative knowledge*, which is knowing about strategy, and *procedural knowledge*, which is knowing how to use a strategy (Paris, Lipson, & Wixson, 1994). Although both types of knowledge are fundamental to strategic actions, neither declarative nor procedural knowledge is sufficient for students to be able to apply strategies. What must be addressed is students' *conditional knowledge*, that is, being able to use a strategy under different conditions (Paris, Wixson, & Palinscar, 1986). Without conditional knowledge, students will only be able to use a strategy when a teacher requests that they use that specific method.

If students are unable to transfer the use of strategies independently, what is the purpose of teaching? When the classroom teacher completes instruction on a specific strategy with a group of students, can we continue to assume that the students learned that strategy to the point where they are able to transfer it and use this instruction independently, at their seats or in their homes? We have taught them what the strategies are (declarative knowledge), and how to use the strategies (procedural knowledge). Why have we not taught conditional knowledge, too?

Learning How to Learn

A process that gradually evolved into double-instructed reading was targeted at students who needed to make more than one year of reading growth during one school year. It is important for students to achieve on their enrolled grade level in reading because reading proficiency spills over into successful learning of all subjects at grade-level standards and affects the quality of students' futures.

Double-instructed reading stems from conditional knowledge research, which is the notion of transfer. In *Understanding by Design*, McTighe and Wiggins (2004) explain that the difference between knowledge and understanding is that understanding is transferable to new contexts. At issue is this consideration: can students use the knowledge and strategies they have been taught by their teachers in new and different situations? For an affirmative answer to this question, instruction has to move beyond declarative and procedural knowledge to impart conditional knowledge (Paris, Lipson, & Wixson, 1994; Vygotsky, 1978); that is, helping students learn how to learn.

The key is relevance. Students need to understand the purpose of a strategy, in addition to being given appropriate situations within which to explore the strategies they learn. The purpose of double-instructed reading is to scaffold instructional support until students are able to transfer understanding under different conditions, such as reading independently and successfully on their enrolled grade level. The benefits are that students become able to apply strategies that help them learn, become self-directed thinkers, and are prepared to accept responsibility for their own learning.

The outcomes of the double-instructed reading process are threefold:

1. The number of students in both the general and special education populations performing below their enrolled grade level is significantly reduced.

2. When teachers are asked the initial Essential Question, "Why are students in your class reading below grade level?," they have the knowledge and understanding to respond. Now, everyone working with the children, including administrators, resource teachers, and the entire grade-level Data Team, can respond, because conversations make the data transparent as they are incorporated during step 1 of the Data Team process. Plus, everyone has access to the student goals indicated on the class student maps and Concern and Action Maps (see Chapter 1) addressing specific needs.

3. The core of double-instructed reading is the notion of students receiving explicit instruction to increase transfer of strategies and skills to the point of demonstrated understanding.

Although the concept of having tutors teach students in a directed model that supports the teacher by doubling the instructional time is not new, we increased the success by the way in which we used our tutors, creating transparency among all our human resources.

Putting Double-Instructed Reading into Action

Double-instructed reading is a structured reading program that provides reading intervention support for struggling readers directly in the classroom. "Mostly we send our struggling kids out of the room for skill and drill and 'corrective' programs, and they miss the valuable instruction they need most" (Routman, 2003, p. 207). "Students need at least a double dose of excellent practice" (Routman, 2003, p. 208). Double-instructed reading is not a fragmented, isolated, boxed program, but a way to provide students who are weak in reading, as determined by formative assessments, with additional "face time" with a teacher-tutor inside the classroom. This tutor scaffolds the classroom teacher's instruction by giving these students more time to practice using and transferring their learnings before they go back to their seats. There are no assumptions here. When these students do return to complete independent assignments, they do not return to their seats having been *taught*, they return having *learned!*

This structured reading process provides students with more than just additional "teacher talk," by focusing on the need for students to be able to transfer learning. It is also an example of how to use data generated by Data Teams to make instructional decisions to support students' progress. In today's climate, in which funds are targeted to the lowest-performing schools, principals of schools that are barely skimming the surface of proficiency need help that does not come with a large price tag.

Finding kids *before* we lose them is a significant responsibility of classroom teachers and administrators. Initially, double-instructed reading was designed for students who were not reading with comprehension on their enrolled grade level. As it turned out, it also provides support for students who are just beginning to read at grade-level standards, but need training wheels occasionally when the going gets wobbly. Just as all students are included in our conversations, they are all entitled to every available human resource. Therefore, special education students and all special needs students benefit as well.

When principals pay for tutors with school funds, rather than district funds, they can use annual school improvement goals as guidelines for tutor support. Teachers determine which students require support because the teachers' professional judgment is respected.

The double-instructed reading process is simple. After the classroom teacher is finished providing small-group instruction to the particular group in need of support, the DIR tutor then provides 45 additional minutes (three times a week) of small-group instruction (Exhibit 3.3), to foster the transfer of the targeted skill in a new context.

EXHIBIT 3.3

The Basic Double-Instructed Reading Process (Classroom Teacher and DIR Tutor)

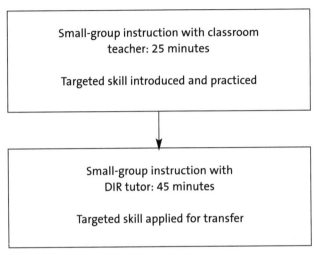

Small-group instruction with classroom teacher: 25 minutes

Targeted skill introduced and practiced

↓

Small-group instruction with DIR tutor: 45 minutes

Targeted skill applied for transfer

Finding Tutors You Can Count On

Finding tutors who have teaching qualifications or experience requires some creativity. The following suggestions help put an end to the fragmented and substandard instruction generally available to our low-performing students.

The faculty resource teachers, such as special education teachers and reading specialists, need to align their instruction with the classroom teacher's instruction. Transparency of responsibilities and fluidity of roles develop between classroom teachers and special needs teachers and enhances the power of the instruction that each child gets. Communication in a conversational culture helps to avoid the current fragmented instructional models under which each specialist provides separate instruction. Increasing the coherence of instruction for struggling readers boosts their potential for understanding and transfer of concepts. In essence, resource teachers can work with the same DIR framework inside the classroom.

Volunteers are not used as tutors. Additional tutors are hired with hourly funds and are trained by our reading specialist. To raise the standards while enlarging the pool of tutors, you may want to consider:

- Retired teachers (everybody's favorite!)
- College students in educational career courses
- Teachers and newly graduated teachers who are looking for a job
- Parents or community members who have some educational coursework

Practicality is important. Remember, a few teacher-tutors go a long way. The tutors only meet with the particular students or reading group three times per week. One tutor can work at several grade levels. This is the opposite of putting our weakest instructors with our struggling students, because every student initially receives small-group instruction on the particular skill directly from the regular classroom teacher. The tutor stays at that teaching point while working with the struggling student. Also, our specialists use the same model, providing more continuity for students as they are promoted between grades.

I have found that the degree of expertise we can get directly correlates with the amount of money we can pay for professional tutors. For example, retired teachers and local college students enrolled in education courses are wonderful tutors. We have found that scheduling a tutor where needed for just three days, for 45 minutes per class, increases students' ability to successfully transfer comprehension and writing skills and strategies to their independent reading and writing. As this transfer ability (or conditional knowledge) grows, students become able to independently transfer to new situations strategies taught to them by the regular classroom teacher. In essence, we help them learn how to learn.

Increasing Fidelity among All Teachers

Opportunities for resource teachers to interconnect their roles with the roles of the classroom teacher lead to transparency and congruence in instruction. "Comprehension accountability makes it clear that teachers and administrators are required to be transparent in their decision making" (Reeves, 2004, p. 121). Instruction that is not fragmented has increased power for students. The same model—having a teacher-tutor providing repeat instruction to students, so that they can learn to the level of being able to transfer their understandings to new situations (see Exhibit 3.3)—is naturally adaptable to the role of reading specialists. Working with children inside the classroom on the same skills and strategies as the classroom teacher increases student success, as described in the following vignette.

 ZOOMING IN ON SUCCESS

"We have more conversations that we would have never had [before]. Sometimes our perspectives are different. If we didn't share our teaching roles, these conversations would never have happened. We have a genuine shared interest in students' growth, but we are not stuck to a 'program.'"

These comments, by Jenny Barnes, explain how her reading specialist role changed by working with students as one of our double-instructed reading tutors. The following is an example of the model described in Exhibit 3.3 with Jenny and a kindergartner after the classroom teacher's instruction.

During a letter identification activity, I highlighted the letters Aine knew. Then Aine asked, "Why are you making those letters blue?"

"I highlighted them because you KNEW them!"

"I know that one, too. Make IT blue!"

She was so obsessed with making letters blue that in four lessons, she knew all the letters of the alphabet!

As Jenny explained, "Whatever matters for the child is what matters most!" What motivated Aine? It was as simple as the color blue. As teachers, we need to collaborate more, be flexible, and tweak what we do to get a good match for kids. This transparency of roles, among those of a classroom teacher, reading specialist, and special education teacher, is a subtle but significant shift in providing instruction—and it requires a conversational culture. "Schools that are more collegial and collaborative are happier places and have higher student achievement. Based on decades of experience, I believe that significant, lasting school change with accompanying higher achievement is not possible without ongoing professional conversations" (Routman, 2003, p. 216).

The aim is for the DIR tutor to teach these students how to transfer the concepts (conditional knowledge) on which they just received instruction from their classroom teacher. Struggling readers generally need more time for learning before they can independently use what they are learning. How do you know when something has been learned? The answer is when "understanding is transferable to new contexts" (McTighe & Wiggins, 1999, p. 8). If they lack the capacity to use the concepts that were taught by the teacher, we can tell that students do not *understand* what they *know*. As Albert, a second-grade student who was working with our DIR tutor said to me, "I'm a better reader because I have fluency." Amazed at his comment, I asked him, "What is fluency?" He said, "I can read smoothly and good now!" The time taken to scaffold the knowledge of concepts into understanding helped this child achieve more than one year's progress. In another year, we hope, he will not be an at-risk reader. With Albert (and others like him), time for instruction was doubled and his class size was reduced for the time the tutor was in his classroom.

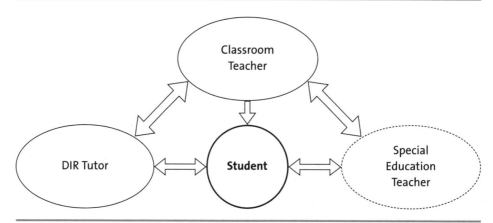

EXHIBIT 3.4 **Double-Instructed Reading Model with Three Levels of Instruction**

The reading tutors had great success working in the classroom during the students' normal literacy block, scaffolding what the teacher had just taught to small groups of students. This method also leads to fidelity of instruction from special education teachers, as depicted in Exhibit 3.4.

 ZOOMING IN ON SUCCESS

Stacey DeColli, a fourth-grade teacher, planned weekly with the special education teacher and the DIR tutor (who in this instance was our reading teacher), to make sure that the IEP goals were met. Stacey explained, "This worked exceptionally well for my students. The three of us were able to provide consistent instruction, instead of fragmented drills on skills."

The reading teacher explained, "My time is counted in" for the required special education IEP hours. Eventually, the DIR tutor time was reduced to provide students with opportunities to read and write independently, so that they could also practice transferring their learning.

"Next year I am recommending that these students be monitored only. I believe they will be ready to maintain their improved growth independently next year without the support of the DIR tutor."

The hallmark of double-instructed reading is flexibility. Stacey DeColli used the model shown in Exhibit 3.4 to integrate her resources teachers. The teachers who share roles in working with a group of students keep a collective journal. For example, one journal entry stated: "Did you notice how much better these students did?"

"We write down our observations and then see trends. When a lesson clicks, you know it. We put that out there too!"

The following is a think-aloud that occurred during a Compelling Conversation between an intermediate teacher and a principal about the best ways the DIR tutor could provide instructional support for five students.

ZOOMING IN ON SUCCESS

"It is exciting that three more of your students are reading on grade level now! Let's think about this together. You will still have two students who are not reading successfully on grade level. What could you do differently with instruction to help these two?"

"Well, I could have our DIR tutor work with just them. What do you think? I mean, I think it is good! It would make the other three students feel good because they do not need support any longer. Then the tutor could work with the two boys who really need more support right now."

"Great strategy. That would really help you determine their needs!"

Looking for Invisible Excellence

In ways not measured with pie charts, or reading levels, or test scores, children move forward. We talk about *Invisible Excellence* in relation to children who may not yet be achieving grade-level standards, but are making *more* than one year's growth during a school year. They may not be on grade level *this* year. However, talking about their growth, recording it on the teacher's student map, and *holding on to the growth over the summer for the next grade* results in more students going to middle and high school capable of reading on grade level and feeling good about themselves during the tough adolescent years. A key component of the big picture of *developing learning success* for kids' future lives is right here: Invisible Excellence.

Invisible Excellence student achievement is a hallmark of Compelling Conversations. These students are a tribute to the new bell curve (Reeves, 2004), which sets high expectations and provides opportunities for *every* student to achieve success. Previously, struggling readers never caught up because they were held captive to the traditional bell curve; "a year for a year" imprisons the potential of children who struggle in the early years. When Compelling Conversations extend beyond the classroom walls into the hearts of teachers, the culture becomes more caring, and these students do not get left behind.

What does Invisible Excellence look like? The model in Exhibit 3.5 depicts inclusion of a special education teacher and a double-instructed reading tutor to provide

◉◉
EXHIBIT 3.5　**Model for Invisible Excellence**

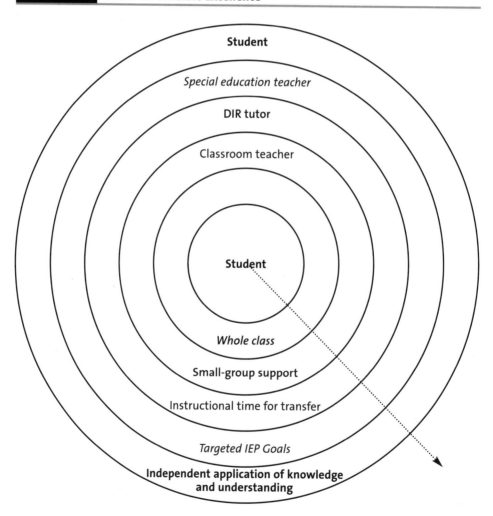

instruction that is transparent between specialists and seamless for students.

Students who receive instruction in this model break out of the bell curve by achieving a range of up to one and a half years' growth in one year. Yet, these students are still not at grade-level standards. These children are not retained; they are not failures. Instead, these students are commended for achieving Invisible Excellence—more than one year's progress in one year. In his conceptualization of Attribution Theory, Marzano (2006) explains that a factor influencing students' effort is the perceived capacity to succeed. Additionally, Tomlinson and McTighe state the need to "reflect consistently on individual or group growth in order to adjust instruction in ways of greatest benefit to individuals and the class as a whole." (2006, p. 54). Therefore, by the next year, if we hold on to the progress made and provide the needed supports, these students will be successful on their grade-level standards and will be on their way to experiencing pride, success, and a joy in learning that will see them through their whole lives.

Some students make 1½ years' growth. Some don't. Some grow 1¼ years. But that's okay because you hold on to that growth, and over two or three years, these students will be successfully learning on their grade level. That's the goal. Invisible Excellence!

Classroom teachers have weekly conversations with the special education teachers and DIR tutors about the "priority needs" of students who need to make more than one year's growth this year. These students' priority needs are typically benchmarks from the previous grade that require additional focus. The teachers provide collaborative instruction inside the classroom based on these needs. One teacher explained that it took months to figure out who was awake in the morning first. Being awake became a priority need! Schedules were juggled for these children, who needed more attention paid to the *timing* of instructional delivery so that it would connect with their learning styles.

After the classroom teacher teaches the small group of struggling students the targeted skills (including reading for comprehension), those students work with the DIR tutor to read and discuss concepts one more time. Two days a week, students work independently and assume responsibility for transferring their understanding. Following reading and discussion of the material, the DIR tutor may do some vocabulary or word work by having students find "chunks" in the vocabulary from their story. These chunks are part of the whole-class spelling words for the week, and the same vocabulary terms are incorporated into writing.

The special education teacher provides services to meet the IEP objectives through writing instruction related to objectives. The same vocabulary and word work are tailored to achieve the students' IEP objectives. Independently, students complete related word-work activities and process writing. Most importantly, they are given time to read. The entire collaborative lesson is planned to provide *increased instructional time* in a *smaller class:* for the time the tutor and resource teachers are in the room, the *class size is greatly reduced.* The conversations among all teachers are focused on connecting and extending the instruction of the classroom teacher, so that these double-instructed students have more opportunities to transfer their learning and achieve more than one year's growth during the current year.

Invisible Excellence arises wherever teachers believe in their children. More than one year's progress in only one year is planned for in September and backward-mapped with goals for each quarter. During our very first Compelling Conversation, the teachers and I talk about what-ifs: "What if we do . . . ?" "Could it be possible for this student to make more than one year's progress this year?" "How can I help you make this happen?" Then, teachers backward-map the June goals in September and plan for the increase in learning each student needs to achieve during each quarter. (Remember that we are planning for students who need to make more than one year's growth to be successful on their grade-level standards.)

When monitoring students' progress during Compelling Conversations, modifications are made and instruction is adjusted. Are we successful in achieving our goals for every child? No. However, for each one of the children who are successful, it matters to them. Sometimes, a student does not achieve the goals—but we did not and do not "lose" this child. We know that this student did not achieve standards, so we continue to monitor progress and make midcourse corrections until the student is successful, as described in the "Learning" quadrant of the Leadership for Learning Framework (Reeves, 2005, p. 133).

We may not ever know the real-life results of our accomplishments. They exist in the future choices our kids will make: peer groups, remaining in school, and how they use their free time. These choices shape students' vital decisions. They determine the quality of students' experiences and affect the length of their lives. For this reason, I extend our passionate concern for kids beyond our school. For example:

> While driving to work, I sometimes see students smoking at the bus stop. I pull my car over and get out, greeting a particular student.
>
> "Hi, Brian. How's it going in middle school?"
>
> "Everything's going pretty good, Dr. Piercy."
>
> "Well, must not be that good, Brian. I see you are smoking now. You know what I'm trying to say? I am concerned about you, Brian. I want

> you to take care of yourself. Do you think you could try to stop smoking? It would mean a lot to me if you could."

Afterward, I do not see the kids smoking when I drive by. Do they light up as soon as I'm gone? I'll never know. They do know that I care and that can't hurt.

When children, teachers, and administrators tap into their talents, passion is fueled. It is then that assessment scores are changed. As the roles of administrators, leaders, classroom teachers, and resource teachers become more transparent, conversations iterate deeply throughout the culture. The voice of the culture becomes deeply embedded in relationships.

The achievement slope of a whole school cannot be changed by focusing on one test. That is backward thinking, which is quite different from backward mapping for results. When a school focuses on the slope of one child, however, the achievement of a school increases. As a secondary effect, not the overarching goal, achievement improves in measurable ways. As a third-grade teacher explained, "I think if George weren't having a double-instructed reading tutor, he would be reading below his grade level. He feels secure and gets to feel confident in comprehension."

Increasing Expectations: On- and Above-Grade-Level Learners

An important aspect of Compelling Conversations is time dedicated to continuous consideration of the degree to which school standards are supporting on- and above-grade-level learners in fulfilling their potential. When students are successfully learning on or above their enrolled grade level, they relish engaging instruction that expands their capabilities beyond vertical growth.

As students become accomplished readers, expectations need to be kept high. Raising expectations does not mean adding more classroom charts of strategies and skills or assigning additional work. Elaborate and extensive research projects that exhaust students do not increase student achievement, as Routman clarified: "Higher-quality work is not by definition long" (Routman, 2005, p. 54). Rather, raising expectations urges students to discover what it means to read with a depth of understanding. Reading well gives students pleasure and self-confidence, which leads to enthusiasm about reading.

Does reading a higher-level book increase students' reading capabilities? Or is their thinking expanded by focusing on conversations with student questioning about rich literature? Differentiation of instruction for our on- and above-grade-level learners is not accomplished by giving students more assignments, but by providing explicit teaching that promotes students' intellectual growth. Teachers respond to learners' needs by adjusting the content taught, processes incorporated, or products expected so that they can observe students in a variety of perspectives, not only as a static or rigid group (McTighe, 2006). The Optimal Learning Model (Routman, 2005) indicates that instruction is at the optimal level for learners when it includes both independent writing and reading opportunities and partner writing and reading, allowing students to initiate, self-monitor, apply learning, problem solve, and confirm. At this level, the teacher affirms, acknowledges, coaches, and incorporates goals. We help students' reading capacity acquire depth when we challenge them to transfer their reading comprehension of a story into writing thoughtfully about a personal connection with the story, a relationship between two different texts, or a link to a world event (Langer, 2002). Accomplished readers need time for horizontal growth in addition to vertical growth, to deepen their learning and extend their understanding. When this student growth is developed into measurable goals, monitored frequently during Compelling Conversations, and shared during the Data Team process, student achievement for all learners increases.

Summary

Compelling Conversations allow the administrative team to contribute to ground-level decisions about students' growth. The student-specific and Data-Team-specific data show which students would benefit from the structured reading process called double-instructed reading. Conversations lead to collaboration throughout the culture, including specialists and administrators; this results in struggling learners receiving support directly in the classroom with models of instruction based on the DIR process. Another result is students' achievement of Invisible Excellence, making more than one year's growth in one academic year. Double-instructed reading is grounded in conditional knowledge research, which explains that *understanding* requires students to be able to transfer knowledge to a new situation. Simply put, "to understand is to be able to use knowledge" (McTighe & Wiggins, 1999, p. 8). As teachers reach out collaboratively by investing in more frequent conversations about students' understanding, communication improves and the entire school culture is altered to align with and support the school's true mission: *student learning.*

CHAPTER 4

CONVERSATIONS: *Communication for Leadership Capacity and Sustainability*

Essential Question: *How can Compelling Conversations establish a culture for a professional learning community that sustains achievement and future change?*

Chapter Foreword   BARB KAPINUS

Usually when one reads about leadership and school change, the focus is on creating visions, lining folks up behind the vision through buy-in, and developing organizational structures. This chapter considers leadership from a different perspective—but one that is at the center of education for everyone. The focus is on *understanding*. The leadership described here is a dance among the understandings teachers have of students, students have of their learning, and principals have of teachers and students. Here is a different view of interacting, for the purpose of understanding and improving rather than managing. My favorite sentence in the chapter is, "The path of sustained change begins face to face, one conversation at a time." This connotes a thoughtful, people-centered approach far different from the one-minute management approach touted in the past.

The leaders profiled in this chapter are *courageous*, willing to be honest about problems and needs. They are *humble*, working side by side with teachers to discern ways to promote learning, rather than issuing directives from cloistered offices. They listen to what teachers say, which both honors and raises the professionalism of teachers. They are *patient*, taking time for real dialogue and recognizing that student achievement grows week by week and month by month in classrooms, sometimes in fits and starts.

The strategies and dispositions described here are important for more than principals and school leaders. They also serve parents in dealing with their children and their children's teachers. They greatly serve the policy makers who should listen more and spend less time spinning new, quick fixes to education challenges. The strategies described here are not just about being caring and understanding, though passion for learning underlies all Compelling Conversations. They do constitute a set of tools for bringing a laser-like focus to the enterprise of schooling, by focusing on student data and progress in very concrete and dedicated ways.

I am privileged to know the author and to have witnessed her growth as an educator. The ideas in this chapter are the nexus of her thoughtfulness, caring, experience, and intelligent analysis.

Introduction

Compelling Conversations establish multiple levels of communication within a school by focusing on student progress. During these conversations, the principal, school leaders, classroom teachers, and resource teachers learn from one another while they are learning about students. As the roles of principal and teacher merge, the staff's capacity for collaboration develops within teams and between grades. Also, the principal emerges as a contributing leader and becomes aware of tipping points that are opportunities to begin changing nonproductive norms. Gradually, multiple forms of professional development shape the culture, supporting the expansion of individual teachers' capacities and assisting the growth of aspiring leaders. Compelling Conversations support progress both in student achievement and in future change.

With the process of conversations extending to all educators responsible for instruction, multiple levels of communication are established, networked, and strengthened, as represented in Exhibit 4.1.

◎◎
EXHIBIT 4.1   **Multiple Levels of Communication**

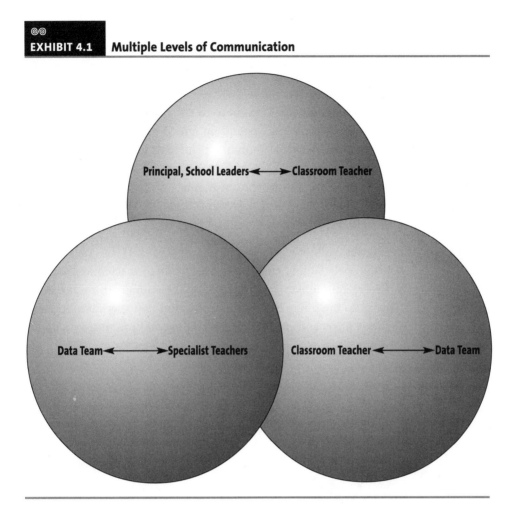

Compelling Conversations: Merging Leadership and Teaching Roles

Getting to a place where the principal and school leaders can sit down with each teacher to share their thoughts about students' learning progress can take a long time. This is because the principal's perspective on teachers' performance has traditionally been from a distance, as the principal observes and evaluates teachers. (There has always been more than a little of the traditional boss–employee relationship between principals and teachers, too, which further hinders open and honest conversation.) Student understanding and progress—the genuine indicators of quality teaching—have remained outside the loop of teacher evaluation, as if there were a red velvet barrier, as in a museum, preventing us from stepping near enough for close inspection—not only of data, but also of the decisions that may yield masterpiece results. Investigation of individual-brushstroke decisions has not been possible from the distant perspective from which administrators usually do evaluations.

As curators of schools, we need to go beyond the protective buffer between teacher performance and student understanding and progress. Mike Schmoker explains that this buffer "ensures [that] building principals know very little about what teachers teach, or how well they teach" (2006, p. 13). These, however, are the primary factors that determine our students' learning and futures. Unintentionally, this buffer deeply limits a school's capacity to effect the highest quality instruction for students.

Perhaps if this buffer had not existed, we would not currently be controlled by the federal government's No Child Left Behind act. The disconnectedness between student progress and accountability is represented in the segmentation of Exhibit 4.2. This figure illustrates the fragmented communication that keeps teacher evaluation, teacher performance, and student understanding and progress as separate arenas.

EXHIBIT 4.2   Fragmented Levels of Communication

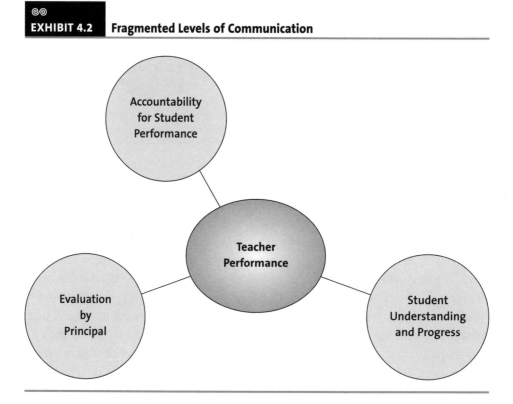

Repairing Fragmented Communication

The resolution needed to repair fragmented communication is apparent: the roles of the teacher and principal have to merge. Establishing connections between these roles adds a level of communication about student understanding and student progress that has not existed previously. It is a natural step, though, considering that an important indicator of quality teaching—student understanding—is also a significant component determining school performance.

Merging the roles of teacher and principal, so that every student's progress can be discussed honestly and fruitfully, is a pivotal step in uniting two key indicators of accountability: (1) student understanding and progress and (2) school performance. Compelling Conversations with every teacher, about every child, held regularly throughout the school year, repair or replace the fragmentary communications about student progress that have been traditional with the principal or school leader (Exhibit 4.3).

Discussing expectations for each student and writing end-of-year goals in September for every student are both part of a concrete first step toward account-

◎◎
EXHIBIT 4.3   **Compelling Conversations Communication Model**

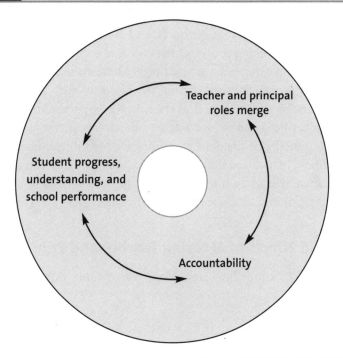

ability. No longer disconnected by dependence on external assessments, accountability becomes real as teachers, principals, and school leaders backward-map the progress of all students, establishing goals for more than one year's growth when necessary. As these goals are assessed each quarter during the regularly scheduled Compelling Conversations, teachers begin to believe that they really can affect each student's progress (see Chapter 1). As student understanding increases, so does the school's overall performance level. Through the assessment of conversations, students' understanding and school performance are connected to accountability that is *shared* (see Chapter 2).

During Compelling Conversations, the teacher, principal, and school leaders learn from each other while learning about students. Most importantly, conversations are enjoyable. These conversations are important because they create professional communities capable of aligning today's students with learning (Garmston & Wellman, 1999). Each time teachers share their opinions with principals and school leaders, trust is mutually strengthened.

Recognizing that Compelling Conversations increase the communication of opinions and feelings explains how traditionally accepted practices, such as testing during the first weeks of school to determine instructional placements for the new school year, also come to be discussed. One main investment that faculties can make to support improved student learning is to develop the staff's capacity for participating in professional conversations (Garmston & Wellman, 1999).

The path of sustained change begins face to face, one conversation at a time. Conversations are reinforcing processes that act as the support beams for continued change and construction of a new culture. These conversations are gripping because they require internal work by the teacher, principal, assistant principal, and school leaders, as each reflects and considers new possibilities. This internal work of thinking critically about decisions by all participants is assisted by focusing on the components of dialogue that improve communication and decision making. *Conditions of dialogue* (Exhibit 4.4) are behaviors that you personally can control to increase effective communication. Effective dialogue, supported with these conditions, promotes collaborative understanding.

The Sustained Effects of Merging Teacher and Principal Roles

Peter Senge stated, "Compelling, new ideas help people think and act in new ways"(1999, p. 44).

- **Suspend assumptions**—Focus on the concept

- **Befriend polarization**—You and I have different ideas, but I will carefully consider your idea

- **Observe the observer**—Look at the body language of people who are *not* talking

- **Listen to your listening**—Think about what your thoughts are

- **Be aware of thought**

- **Slow down inquiry**—Slow down your questions (you may not have really listened to an answer if you are peppering others with queries)

- **Respect all views**

- **Address issues, not people**

- **Avoid arguing for your position**—Start by questioning, then listen to other ideas

- **Present your position logically, then listen**

- **Do not change your mind just to avoid conflict**

- **Differences of opinions are natural and to be expected**—Many times, these divergences create the best possibilities for change and fresh perspectives

Three Cornerstones for Learning

According to Senge, the three cornerstones of the most effective initiatives that create an environment for learning are: guiding ideas, infrastructure, and theories and methods.

Guiding Ideas. Implementation of the Compelling Conversations concept does not require significant funds from ever-tightening school budgets. The conversations are held openly by all staff members, and student results are discussed with parents. The need for relevance is significant (Reeves, 2004; Routman, 2005). Conversations do not stop after the meetings scheduled for them are over; they continue in an uninterrupted dialogue throughout the school day. Teachers have the locus of control because the changes that can result from Compelling Conversations are in their hands. The clearest indicator of teachers' direct control over changes in student achievement is their capacity to know the learner so well that their Compelling Conversations have predictive qualities regarding high-stakes assessments.

Answers to previously unasked questions are recognized during Compelling Conversations:

■■ *What if teachers could predict each of their students' performance outcomes on state-level high-stakes assessments?*

   Imagine the instructional choices that could be made if teachers recognized that their professional decisions had predictive qualities regarding student achievement, as measured by state assessments.

■■ *How about if teachers, principals, and students knew these predictions during the school year?*

   If teachers knew which students would not be achieving proficiency by the end of the year, could that help them to adjust their instructional choices accordingly during the year?

A clear correlation and connection exist between teachers' judgment of the level at which their students are successfully learning with understanding (as discussed and documented during collaborative Compelling Conversations) and the outcomes on high-stakes assessments. The children are in good hands when their teachers know them as learners this well (Piercy, 2000).

Infrastructure. The practice of having regularly scheduled conversations that are not conducted during planning time or after school, but on the clock, constitutes a significant infrastructure change. To ensure that conversations with every classroom teacher take place, the new practice of reserving one day each quarter to meet with individual teachers is included on the yearly school calendar. During these initial conversations, end-of-year goals for each student are collaboratively generated. Also, as discussed in Chapter 2, Data Teams meet, in what are sometimes referred to as "Team Huddles" (Schmoker, 2001), to use the data generated during Compelling Conversations.

The measure of student progress is the data pie charts generated during conversations; these are dramatic evidence that teachers are the experts. Motivated by possibilities, teachers team-teach, increase standards for specific students in the time between conversations, informally assess more frequently, and offer informative meetings and workshops for parents.

Theories and Methods. Foundational to the Compelling Conversations process is the backward-design concept described in *Understanding by Design* (McTighe & Wiggins, 2004) for integrating questioning, standards, and accountability. As Schmoker states, "teacher expertise is one of the most grossly underused assets in education" (2001, p. 1). When these concepts are integrated into collaborative, professional learning communities (Eaker, Dufour, & Dufour, 2002), rich potential exists for conversations that make a significant difference in teacher capacity. The merging of the teacher and principal roles in the Compelling Conversations process demonstrates high regard and respect for teacher expertise. Furthermore, the data garnered both support and further the significant work done during the Data Teams process (2006; The Leadership and Learning Center, formerly Center for Performance Assessment).

The principal signs the report card, too. Principals are equally accountable for every student.

The direct connection between teachers' judgment of students' instructional level and students' actual performance is strengthened during Compelling Conversations, because our collaboration helps us to notice small changes in students' achievement. A distinguishing characteristic of a tipping point is that "little causes or changes can have big effects" (Gladwell, 2005, p. 9). When students are either not challenged, not successful, or both, everyone on the Data Team knows it, and they collaboratively make modifications to accommodate those students.

Accountability is transparent because the teacher, entire team, principal and assistant principal, and students know their goals and current progress toward those goals over time. This is the frame for what Douglas Reeves termed "holistic accountability" (Reeves, 2004). Anxiety about state assessments is replaced with confidence underlined with anticipation, because there are no surprises. The "unknown" is not the assessment scores that arrive after students and teachers are gone for the summer, but the facts revealed during Compelling Conversations: Which students are in need of help to achieve standards, and how can we provide immediate support that is aligned with their needs? A student's classroom performance is focused on the process of understanding. The daily instructional level is the crucial connection. The level at which the teacher delivers instruction is the point where accountability and state assessments connect directly with student understanding.

By stepping into the picture of instructional decisions about individual student progress, through Compelling Conversations, a principal becomes a contributing leader. As accountability is bridged between the teacher and principal, beliefs are bolstered with courage and instruction becomes intentional.

Becoming a Contributing Leader

It has been uncomfortable being an unknowing instructional leader. Aspiring to work with teachers in areas that include curriculum, instruction, and assessment issues, which are all important components of being an instructional leader

(Robbins & Alvy, 2004), has been challenging. High school principals have had a most challenging task of integrating the instructional-leader model, as Joanne describes in the following.

ZOOMING IN ON SUCCESS

Joanne was the principal of a blue-ribbon school. While we walked down the hallway together, students constantly stopped Joanne to exchange a few humorous comments.

"How are you, as the instructional leader, able to improve the quality of instruction by such a large, diverse faculty?"

"I can't do it personally. I am not an expert in geometry, chemistry, or music. What I can do is hire the finest teachers available and support them in attending excellent professional development activities."

I recognized the discomfort experienced by an instructional leader who could not possibly possess expertise in all the numerous content areas. As a contributing leader, I know that I do not know—but I talk about it. The focus of conversations with teachers is not what I know, but what students are learning.

Shedding the all-knowing image associated with instructional leaders provides opportunities to contribute at a different level, the ground level. It is from the ground level that questions of essential importance arise. Essential Questions related to leadership come from subtle awareness of an invisible norm that may peek its head only briefly into a conversation. In these conversations, trust is emerging. Carefully balancing conversations within the continuum of being non-threatening and rigorous, leaders establish the potential for better instruction that can result in raising the standards, which "describe the knowledge we expect all student to learn" (Routman, 2000, p. 4). Move gently as you interconnect with vulnerable teachers' thoughts!

New Leadership Model:
Instructional Leader to Contributing Leader

Discussing students and their progress during a conversation with a teacher removes the principal and assistant principal from the "I've got all the answers" instructional leader's pedestal. This is quite a change in approach. In the conversations model, the responsibility for student learning within the teacher role and the authoritative problem-solving principal role merge. During Compelling Conversations, the merging of these roles runs directly counter to the way teachers are used to making decisions, as well as how principals have traditionally spent their time. Also, the new model opposes the natural drive of leaders in education to take care of problems, and to do it fast. In fact, changing the approach to leadership changes how a school runs in numerous ways, including perspectives about authority, problem-solving processes, accountability responsibilities, reduced anxiety about student performance, and increased collegiality.

With federal legislation and mandates increasing, the pressure for principals and other administrators to become more directive and controlling leaders has grown. Changing the approach from instructional leadership to contributing leadership provides opportunities to collaborate with teachers to solve problems—a powerful approach that achieves remarkable results. Will you see results overnight? No. You're not supposed to! These changes create results that penetrate deeply into the core of teaching and the school culture. Individual conversations with teachers about each and every student lead to Data Team conversations, the setting of better and more intelligent goals, and the use of collaborative strategies to reach those goals. Reflection continuously refines the process. Yes, the teacher is accountable for the year's growth, but let's not overlook the fact that the principal's name is also on each report card.

Accountability is shared as principals fully use the human and time resources available to a school to develop problem-solving options. There are no surprises when the much-delayed high-stakes state test results are dramatically released by the state directly to the press. Reading about your school's and district's progress in the newspaper first is like students and parents receiving report-card grades in the school newsletter. Increased anxiety is *not* an antecedent of school improvement. The point is that increased direct communication improves achievement. Compelling Conversations extinguish fear, as teachers' confidence snowballs into energy and excitement about students' progress. Teachers know their learners. Their frequent monitoring of student progress negates the possibility of surprises when state assessments are released, because teachers have already predicted the students' high outcomes—quite accurately.

Time that teachers can count on to meet with the administrative team again helps to reassure teachers of our commitment. The teachers get to know the administrative team differently. Actually, they get to know us! Of what use is a leadership model that requires professional learning communities if the principal, assistant principal, and teacher roles remain disconnected? Time with our teachers is greatly needed because

How can we learn more about these students than data can tell us?

These days, enrolling students have needs we've never considered. Today you may enroll a family from Bangkok. Yesterday, you may have entered a student who was blind. More than ever before, all educators need dedicated time for structured conversation.

they are the ones who really know what is happening. Honestly, even as a principal with the heart of a teacher, I know that I can never really be at the coal face; that joy is experienced only by teachers. Administrators can, however, get down in the mine and participate with teachers during our special time for Compelling Conversations.

The suggestion that principals and school leaders change from their directive approach to one of shared problem solving with staff cuts against the current climate. The pressure on the principal for all students to be successful coincides with increased enrollment of public-school students who do not speak English. The students to whom I am referring here are not the ones who speak English as a second language, or even English-language learners (ELLs), but students who do not speak English *at all*. Despite enrolling students from multiple countries, whose concerns include having no U.S. records, no English-language speaking capability by anyone in the family, and no preparation (not even having a pencil), these students are expected to perform proficiently in one year in core subjects. It may have never been more apparent than now that the approach to leadership must change if the education of all America's students is to remain a societal goal and a symbol of freedom.

If you are still thinking that having focused conversations with each teacher is utterly impossible, I understand. But consider: The principalship *is* the only juncture at which data about every enrolled student's progress converge with the financial resources and human potential available to the school. Gladwell (2002) explains that a bedrock belief that change is possible must underlie successful change efforts. At times, a shift in thinking is required to create new possibilities. Merging roles, during Compelling Conversations about decisions for student progress, results in increased and sustainable achievement.

Invisible Norms Become Tipping Points

Conversations with teachers about student progress gradually uncover decisions that previously were made in isolation (Piercy, 2003). A small portal, which widens as trust evolves with additional conversations, is opened directly onto the invisible norms. The Compelling Conversation process creates a vital transparency between the "people at the coal face and the top management" (Fullen, 2001, p. 91). Having personal conversations with teachers about heartfelt passions changes dynamics in positive ways. These conversations establish a new level of respect and generate very creative solutions. We work together more closely and talk with one another about issues that formerly might have been perceived as unimportant in the typically rushed teacher's school day. Remember, though, teachers are our experts in the field. The principal, assistant principal, school leaders, and teachers all support the vision of the school, but it is the teachers who usually provide the best suggestions to meet the everyday demands. Really, only teachers can, because they are the people who are closest to the daily decision points.

Close proximity can, however, create barriers to perceiving the long-term, cause-and-effect nature of instructional decisions. Conversations shed light on decisions, providing opportunities for reflection and change. To become aware of the invisible decisions that result in

Each conversation is a place where the whole of the culture is represented.

some students either achieving below their capacity or not working up to their full potential, the principal or school leaders must realize that Essential Questions exist throughout the school, just waiting to be asked.

What Does Integration Mean?

At one school, a fifth-grade teacher was providing reading instruction from the same literature book to all 26 students in her class. This was not a read-aloud where the teacher read to students. Having just completed a conversation with this teacher and the administrative team, the assistant principal recognized a discrepancy of two years between the instructional levels of the students and the level of the text from which the teacher was observed providing instruction during a walkthrough. The Essential Question, although begging to be asked, was posed with reflective inquiry.

> ASSISTANT PRINCIPAL: "I noticed that your students were receiving instruction from a book that is not on their instructional levels. For some students, there is a two-year discrepancy. What was your thinking about this decision?"

> TEACHER: "We are studying Philadelphia in social studies. I always use this book on Ben Franklin for reading instruction when I teach the Philadelphia unit. Doesn't our school system believe in the concept of integration anymore?"

> The assistant principal was momentarily stopped! This veteran teacher's spontaneous, honest comments made the assistant principal aware that

outdated folders of materials were being used for instruction, despite the current data available about students' individual instructional needs in reading.

It is at moments precisely like this that "tipping points" (Gladwell, 2002) occur; decisions made at these points have the potential to elevate the school's standards. A *tipping point* is the name given to that moment when change can occur all at once. Having the insight to recognize this as a tipping point gave the assistant principal leverage to actually begin to change this norm, or standard, despite the fact that changing a norm often takes years. The ability to spot a tipping point the moment it jumps out of the shadows into the reality of an otherwise typical day is a valuable asset for a leadership team. Compelling Conversations provide a lens through which tipping points can be revealed and recognized.

Several options for the assistant principal in the preceding example were available. One response could have been to respond immediately, out of frustration: "Integration and sound instruction are not opposing constructs! Does integration mean disregarding the provision of sound reading instruction?" Fortunately, because he recognized this moment as a tipping point at which changing an invisible norm about instruction was possible, the assistant principal chose to stop by after school to continue the conversation with this teacher. His reflective dialogue centered around the following questions:

> "I was thinking about your decision. Do you consider all of your students to be reading on the same instructional level?"

> "How would students' previous assessment records and their current achievement levels support your decision?"

> "To continue with your current instruction would mean that the information you just provided on your student map [see Exhibit 1.12] would have to be changed to indicate that you are providing instruction to some of your students below last year's achievement levels. Are you sure that's what you want to do?"

Why were these particular questions asked? Invisible decisions are not only imperceptible to the leadership team, but can also be undetectable to the very teacher who is making the decision. Buried beneath layers of acceptable practice norms, teacher decisions can be made unintentionally—by default, in a sense. It can also be difficult for a teacher to perceive the long-term effects of inadvertent decisions. These questions created an opportunity for the teacher to reflect on and understand the effects of the decisions. Leaders who use the Compelling Conversations framework create opportunities to access these kinds of instructional choices, which are typically invisible to both the administrative team and the teacher. In a conversational culture, natural opportunities arise to provide individualized professional development for teachers during conversations.

What Does Review Mean?

Another administrator described one of the last conversations scheduled for the end of the year. A teacher stated, "I am not going to be writing down that these two boys will begin at the next level in August. Instead, I am going to write that the recommended level for next year should be the same level they have been at since March of this year." Most often, this sort of recommendation is summed up in one word next to a child's name: "review."

What does *review* mean? Its meaning depends completely on the teacher's interpretation. This type of one-word note has resulted in some students being placed half a year behind or below grade-level standards.

The administrator questioned how it was possible for students to make steady progress all year, as documented with data, and yet not make a year's progress. The administrator did not pose this Essential Question directly to the teacher, though. Instead, reflective inquiry proceeded with: "Why would holding these students back in their reading levels be in their best interest?" The teacher explained that she thought the two particular students' growth in her class was due to the additional support they had received. The administrator knew that tutors do not provide support for the moment, but for sustaining the transfer of concepts to different situations in the future—and data indicate that students do maintain their growth. Nevertheless, the administrator did not discount these conversations. Being accountable for decisions to next year's colleagues was of great importance for this teacher, as it should be.

This teacher's conversation was a tipping point: the administrator realized that students can show growth all year, yet be held back at the end of the year

The beginning of the year is when teachers may say, "I had to drop these students back six months because they forgot a lot over the summer." Try responding to this norm-based question by saying, "Hold on to the students' growth but work on the specific weak skills to return them to the level they had been."

by one isolated decision! Principals and administrative teams are typically not aware when decisions like this occur. Who would think that some students can make much growth, as documented by formal assessments, but still be recommended for a lower level of instruction? This independent decision is another example of fragmented communication, a root cause of students' progress not reflecting their capabilities.

To support improved communication, new standards can be established. The following question should be asked during all conversations, but definitely by the midpoint of the year: "Are there any students who are NOT making *independent* progress toward one full year's growth at this time?" A reflective question, preventive in nature, focuses like a laser directly onto accountability that is student-centered.

Reading tutors return full responsibility for transferring information to students at least one month prior to the closing of school, to ensure that the growth made by students can be maintained independently. This is an indicator of students' capacity to transfer understandings.

The grade-level data pie chart from the June Compelling Conversation is copied (rolled up like a baton and tied with a blue ribbon, if you like) to be handed to the next grade level at the first faculty meeting of the new school year. This is the next grade's incoming data from which goals are written. This level of performance is expected to be maintained to prevent the baton of growth from being dropped over the summer.

Will some teachers say that some students forgot everything over the summer and need to be dropped back several instructional levels? Yes. When they do, be glad. This statement is actually an invitation for you to step beyond the red-velvet barrier to ask: What indicators are there that this student demonstrated success last year? Are there assessments, report-card grades, and work samples? If this is the same student, chances are that the knowledge still exists. A pre-assessment would determine whether the student needs a focused review on specific subskills.

Will teachers comment that they do not believe the recommendations from last year's teacher? Oh, yes. You can count on this. In each conversation, the whole of the culture is reflected, as in a hologram. This question may indicate minimal collegial trust. As trust and respect are increased through the work of the Data Teams, including vertical teaming processes, and professional learning community values, teachers acquire understanding that gradually reduces the frequency of this question. A reply could be, "You need to have this conversation with last year's teacher." Generally, this is a difficult conversation for teachers, and at first an administrator may be requested to attend. As the culture acquires qualities of deeper conversation, though, the awkwardness of such a conversation is replaced with respect for high standards and expectations. Eventually, teachers have conversations quite naturally with the previous year's teacher, *before* our first scheduled Compelling Conversations.

"Positive emotions like happiness and alertness are states in which we don't need attention to ruminate and feel sorry for ourselves" (Csikszentmihalyi, 1997, p. 29). Compelling Conversations provide the principal with enormous "alertness" potential, so as to promote a positive, energized culture for discussing any teacher concerns. A desired result of conversations is that they inform the administrative team of priority areas in need of professional development. The information required may exceed what is listed in the school improvement plan, which typically is required to be completed before the new school year begins, before the new student enrollment takes shape, and before new teachers are hired.

Professional Development Leads to Accountability

Given the importance of the principal in determining both the effectiveness of a school and the success of a school improvement effort, it is not surprising to find that the principal and administrative team also play the major role in determining the ultimate value of a professional development program. A culture shaped by Compelling Conversations leads to the new professional development structures of individualized professional development, leadership development for team leaders and aspiring leaders, team learning groups, and collaborative resource teams, as well as the biweekly staff development model described in Chapter 2.

During conversations, when teachers have difficulty articulating the kinds of instructional strategies they need to provide students, it sends a message that a specific direction or type of staff development is needed.

Individualized Professional Development

Each conversation with every individual teacher is an opportunity to provide one-on-one professional development. The previous section discussed the fact that time for conversation with teachers provides the administrative team with opportunities to guide each teacher toward increased understanding about instructional decisions. For example, we noted that a year's achievement growth for a student can be jeopardized when long-term instruction is provided at a frustration level. Typically, it is difficult for that loss to be regained; thus, a student may continue to function below capacity well into the future.

The "cycle of inquiry" components of questions (Lambert, 2003) include evidence, reflections, and actions; by incorporating these components, the teacher and administrative team can collaboratively determine that the integration of science concepts during reading, for example, should proceed as long as students receive directed reading instruction on their appropriate instructional levels. Student maps are recognized as a source of data transparency and shared accountability as data are increasingly discussed among team members. When leadership is connected to learning, anxiety regarding accountability is greatly reduced (Lieberman & Wood, 2001).

Instead of rolling your eyes and thinking, "Oh my, this teacher does not understand these concepts," realize this teacher reflects the presence of the culture demonstrating what staff development needs exist.

The traditional role of the principal has not tapped into the opportunities for professional development that exist in regular conversations with every teacher. Most teachers recognize "teachable moments," when they need to deviate momentarily from the lesson plan to provide just-in-time instruction. Similarly, Compelling Conversations provide a frame for just-in-time professional development. To encourage and support the development of a professional learning community (Eaker, Dufour, & Dufour, 2002), principals initiate collaborative opportunities and provide professional development as needed during conversations with teachers. This is utterly different from the hoary old check-mark evaluations because Compelling Conversations are a moment of *shared* understanding, as teachers and the administrative team collaboratively wrap their commitment around decisions to help each student.

Misconceptions, such as the intended purpose of integration, are often difficult to detect because they remain hidden behind unquestioned, uninvestigated, buffered assumptions and conventional practices (McTighe & Wiggins, 2004). Teachers, like students, benefit from having more than the traditional snapshot observation. Conversations mediate learning and address needs so that teachers can be guided through their zone of proximal development (Vygotsky, 1978) into the next stage of growth to which they are ready to progress. At that time, Data Teams can raise the level of all teachers' zones of development.

Team Leader Professional Development

The team leaders are the torchbearers for the school. They are the ones who carry the torch of beliefs back to the teams, where it will be held high or dropped. Just as faculty meetings should be devoted to teamwork, monthly Data Team leader meetings should focus on leadership capacity development. Informational items are included—at the end of the meeting. Of course, there are times, such as the end of the year, when the entire meeting has to be managerial. Nevertheless, in a learning community dependent upon collaboration, it is vital for the principal to use the time allocated for Data Team leaders as a precious opportunity to develop leadership capacity.

Through meetings designed for and focused on leadership conversations, Data Team leaders experience expansion of their personal capacity and learn how they can do the same in their team meetings. The Data Team leader meetings prepare these leaders to follow the same model to develop capacity within their teams. Complete with agendas and handouts that may include PowerPoint slides, the model that develops good Data Team leaders also contains powerful potential to expand beliefs of the Data Team members as well. Models for open, honest communication that include the conditions of dialogue (Exhibit 4.4), collection and charting of data assessment results (Exhibit 4.5), and models for backward mapping based on *Understanding by Design* (McTighe & Wiggins, 2004) (Exhibit 4.6) are some structures discussed and implemented during Data Team leader meetings.

Steadfast commitment to leadership requires consistency. Teachers lead supersized lives. Their responsibility for students reaching their potential—not only in achievement areas, but also in character—is all-consuming. Addition of a team leadership role to their already loaded plates must be accompanied with concrete support so that leaders can actively transfer the conditions of leadership to their grade-level team meetings. The two levels of team leader support are procedural and structural.

Procedural Support for Team Leaders. Data Team leaders benefit from having a frame of reference when planning team meetings. This framework is provided by a design for interactive meetings that incorporate vertical team conversations. Powerful conversations occur when our meetings are held in the computer lab using a PowerPoint presentation. This surprised me because I had assumed that having screens would interfere with the visually open space needed for collaborative conversations. In fact, the opposite was true! More dialogue occurred in the computer lab. Our administrative team thinks two factors may be at work here. Computer stations create additional physical "comfort zone" space that may support conditions for dialogue. Also, each Data Team leader has a personal computer screen directly in front of his or her eyes, instead of having to look at a distant wall. The reflective questions or message within the slide are more intensely focused because each team leader has close proximity to his or her own

◎◎
EXHIBIT 4.5 **Collecting and Charting Assessment Progress**

First Semester:

Holistic Assessment Data for GRADES

	Advanced:	Proficient:	Basic:
Grade Level:			
Total (%)			

Percentage of students in GRADE(S) _____ achieving

Proficient & Above: _____

Percentage of students in GRADE(S) _____ achieving

Basic & Below: _____

◎◎
EXHIBIT 4.6 **Backward-Design Framework**

The backward-design approach (McTighe & Wiggins, 2004) consists of three general stages:

1. **Identify Desired Results**

    ↓

2. **Determine Acceptable Evidence**

    ↓

3. **Plan Learning Experiences and Instruction**

screen. Examples of two frames that guide Data Team leaders' conversations include: (1) reflective inquiry about goals, and (2) Essential Questions for team leaders (Exhibit 4.7).

Data Team leaders have the most demanding schedules in the school. Everything a principal can do to support them, even seemingly insignificant things, positively affects many aspects of school. Repeating the same foundational messages at each Data Team leader meeting helps them retain their focus on school and team purposes. Examples of items that may be included are the school goals, the team leaders' mission, the Essential Questions listed in Exhibit 4.7, and DuFour's three general questions (DuFour, 2002):

1. What do we want students to learn?

2. How will we know if they have learned it?

3. What are we going to do if they do not learn it?

◉◉ EXHIBIT 4.7	**Sample PowerPoint Frames to Develop Leadership Capacity for Data Team Leaders**

Frame 1. Reflective Inquiry about Goals

Ongoing exploration of Essential Questions with colleagues will support our professional learning community (PLC). Our responses to three questions (DuFour, 2002) build a common ground of shared knowledge required for a solid foundation of school improvement.

1. What does each team want every student to learn?

2. How will your team know when every student has learned it?

3. How will your team (and our PLC) respond when a student experiences difficulty in learning?

Frame 2. Essential Questions for Data Team Leaders

How do DuFour's three questions support our Essential Questions for conversations about learning?

Data Team Leaders' Essential Questions:

- How can conversations regularly scheduled with your team affect every student's proficiency?
- How can your Data Team conversations establish grade-level connections between state standards, accountability, and increased achievement?
- How can monthly Data Team goals increase effectiveness by including data from Compelling Conversations?

Our meetings result in rich vertical team dialogue and reflection that establish the bedrock for expanding leadership capacity. Data Team leaders can then use the PowerPoint slides (or frames from them) to organize and focus their team meetings.

Structural Support for Team Leaders. To support Data Team leaders in their planning of Data Team meetings, so that conversations have the opportunity to expand the teams' capacity, the following structures are recommended:

Time   Use of a rotating substitute provides each Data Team leader with planning time each quarter. The length of planning time depends on the number of team leaders in your school. One or two hours is not enough, but any amount of time that can be provided demonstrates that the principal considers this leadership role a priority.

Shared Leadership   Typically, there are two Data Team leaders for each team. Sharing the leadership promotes conversations with and support for both leaders. It also increases leadership capacity within the faculty, because all leaders attend the monthly Data Team leader meeting and school improvement meetings.

Team Meetings   Team meetings are scheduled two or three times a month: the first is the faculty meeting dedicated to team goal setting; the second is a Data Team meeting. These are required meetings; however, as the collab-

---

◎◎
EXHIBIT 4.8   **Targeted Teamwork Guidebook**

Targeted Teamwork

School:
Principal:

200___ – 200___

orative nature of the school culture develops, meetings tend to occur weekly and sometimes daily, as team members use lunch or planning time to continue their engaging professional conversations about students.

Targeted Teamwork Guidebooks Every Data Team leader is provided with a guidebook (Exhibit 4.8) containing supportive frameworks for leadership that help busy teachers to efficiently organize team meetings. These frameworks include:

- ▪▪ Data Team handbooks containing the five steps of the Data Team process (See Chapter 2, p. 65, and Exhibit 4.10)

- ▪▪ Guidelines for organizing the monthly/marking-period lunch-hour meetings (Exhibit 4.9)

- ▪▪ Data Team Tool Kit (Exhibit 4.10)

- ▪▪ Goal frames and Data Team data, as discussed in Chapter 2

⊚⊚
EXHIBIT 4.9 **Lunch-Hour Meetings**

Lunch-Hour Team Meeting

This review (for team leaders) may help you focus your lunch-hour team meeting.

1. To establish an **end-of-year goal** for the number of students in your grade who will be reading on their enrolled grade level, use the goal frame. Use the following to determine your goal:

   - The external school data from the state assessment data packets from our last School Improvement Team (SIT) meeting will *generally* guide your goals.

   - The Compelling Conversations student maps are *your* internal data based on *your* team's conversations.

The two pie charts depict:

   - How many students were reading on their enrolled grade level in September

   - How many students are projected to be reading on their enrolled grade level in June

2. To establish the **team focus** for this month's Data Team goal, look at our most recent conversation data, student work samples for each class, and school assessments.

I hope this supports your team. Let us know if we can do anything else to help out.

EXHIBIT 4.10   Data Team Tool Kit

Data Team Leaders Meeting Preparation Guide

Data Team Tool Kit

Bring and refer to these during your Team Huddles:

1. This year's school improvement goal statements
2. Your team's annual goal statement for this year
3. Current Data Team monthly goal
4. Next month's Data Team goal frame
5. Student work, assessments, etc. for targeted obstacles
6. Targeted Teamwork notebook

Data Team Tasks

1. Find the data: "Treasure Hunt"
2. Collect and chart data
3. Analyze strengths and obstacles (to prioritize needs)
4. Establish goals: set, review, revise
5. Select instructional strategies
6. Determine results indicators

Conversations are the foundation of collaboration. One conversation with a teacher and administrative team spirals into the teacher's team. The team has the opportunity to make a commanding difference in the lives of students through its collective energy, which influences the standards of every teacher on the team and raises expectations for all students. A life force of power resides in the team leader's role!

Aspiring Leaders

Aspiring leaders are teachers who have established the personal goal of becoming educational leaders. As conversations about student achievement become deeply woven into the school culture, leadership roles are assumed by more teachers. As standards of student and teacher performance are increased yearly, the number of aspiring leaders also increases. Interesting, isn't it? Each year, when some of our aspiring leaders are appointed to district-level leadership positions, additional teachers step up to the aspiring-leader plate.

I personally feel responsible for helping our staff members achieve their dreams, many of which have to do with leadership. I am *not* responsible for these staff members achieving their dreams—they accomplish their goals themselves—but I do everything possible to support them in their endeavors. Even our students become school leaders through our "Cardinal Companions" program for welcoming new students (designed by our exceedingly competent counselor, Ann Horner).

The responsibility of supporting staff members' achievement of their goals can lead to the provision of direct staff development for those desiring leadership roles. Texts, conversations, and school-based workshops, such as incorporating Stephen Covey's habits, can support leaders as they strive to achieve their professional goals.

Vertical and Grade-Level Conversational Learning Groups

Professional development is directly connected to school improvement. To meet a staff's needs, especially with the increasing number of nontenured teachers, it is necessary to carve time out of *regular* school days to provide vital professional development. Conversational learning groups are a structure for school-based professional development that occurs during the regular school day. Designed around a team of floating substitutes who release either a grade-level team or a vertical team (one representative from each grade, specialist team, and special education team), conversational learning groups focus on one specific topic set by the school improvement team. Conversational learning groups are amazingly powerful because their small size is conducive to conversations, which expands the integration of Compelling Conversations as part of the bedrock culture—as indicated in the following overview of a recent conversational learning group.

Conversational Learning Group:

Topic: Supporting our school improvement plan, we recently provided a learning group on "Writing Essentials: Raising Expectations and Results While Simplifying Teaching."

[See Exhibit 4.11 for a sample agenda and desired outcomes for school improvement].

EXHIBIT 4.11 **Conversational Learning Group Sample Agenda and Desired Outcomes**

School Improvement Team (SIT) Desired Outcome, Purpose, Benefits:

SIT Desired Outcome

_____% or more of our students will read and write proficiently as measured on the state assessment for 200_–200_.

Purpose:

We will explore and determine our beliefs and understandings about _____ in support of our _____ achievement goal.

Benefits:

As a result of this conversational learning group, students will be able to

_____.

AGENDA

Welcome

Belief Statements: Focus on areas of student strengths and areas needing improvement

Let the Journey Begin

[insert title and purpose of topic]

Celebrations

Closure/Feedback

DESIRED OUTCOME: Students will write proficiently with joy and confidence.

TEXT: *Writing Essentials* (Routman, 2005). Teachers read Chapters 2 and 3 before the learning group meets.

Aspiring Leaders Connections: Stephen Covey's (2004) and Regie Routman's (2005) concepts about voice were integrated to enhance conversation and understanding.

Collaborative Models

Collaborative models of professional development (discussed in Chapter 3) develop as a natural outcome of Compelling Conversations. The network of conversations that began between teachers and the principal flowed into grade-level teams and expanded into resource teams that iterated higher standards deeply into the culture. As teachers and resource teachers (reading and special education specialists) began shifting their roles for delivering instruction, the resource teachers talked about the different models being used in other grades, thereby cross-pollinating collaborative models on all grade levels.

The network of conversations creates a closely interconnected culture. Parents also benefited from the collaborative conversations that radiated into the community. One example was the emergence of "Beach Bag Literacy" (Exhibit 4.12), a parent enrichment evening designed to provide parents with instructional tools and a book to read to their child over the summer. The success of Beach Bag Literacy was evident in the number of participants, which increased from the usual 20 or so to more than 350. This evening was planned by a team under the leadership of Jenny Barnes. Her collaborative conversations led to strong rapport between teams; teachers from every grade level supported the event even though it took place during the very busy final weeks of school.

Compelling Conversations insert change deep within the school culture (Exhibit 4.13). They surface visibly as new forms of instructional models, parent connections, and increased student learning evidenced in triangulated measures of achievement that is sustained. "Leaders are not islands in time. By design or default, leadership stands on the shoulders of those who went before and lays the groundwork for those who will follow" (Hargreaves, 2006, p. 4). Compelling Conversations are a foundation for sustained and continued improvement.

⊚⊚
EXHIBIT 4.12   Beach Bag Literacy (Sample Parent Invitation)

Beach Bag Literacy Splash! – Bring the Children!

Stop by to get your free Beach Bag! Talk with teachers from your child's grade level while filling your Beach Bag with grade-appropriate reading strategies, a book, and reading tools that you can use while reading with your children over the summer. There is no meeting or starting time. Please come at your convenience between _____ and _____ on _____, _____, 200__.

Thank you for starting your summer vacation with reading!

◎◎
EXHIBIT 4.13   **Growth Processes for Compelling Change**

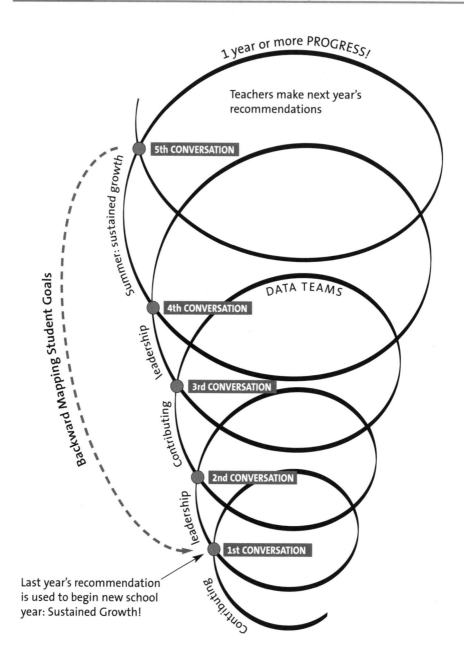

Summary

Compelling Conversations expand the culture of a professional learning community by establishing multiple levels of communication that did not previously exist. Time teachers can count on to talk with the administrative team every month or marking period allows us all to learn from one another while learning about students. Through regular conversations about students' progress in achieving their personal goals, the roles of the teacher and principal or school leader merge; this is a pivotal occurrence that unites student understanding and progress with school performance. The assessment of student progress data that results from the conversations is connected to accountability that is shared by all stakeholders: principal, school leaders, teachers, and Data Team members. Changing the approach to leadership, from the instructional-leader model to the contributing-leader approach, changes how a school is run and necessarily effects deep change in the school's culture. From perspectives about authority, problem-solving processes, accountability responsibilities, reduction of unknowns about assessments (and reduction of the related anxiety), and increased collegiality through staff development, the contributing-leader model effects change that is connected to measurable, sustainable student achievement across various school cultures. Compelling Conversations are a natural next step for an evolving professional learning community. Because conversations let us step inside the barriers between student progress and teaching quality for a closer look (eliminating the buffer), the connecting link of Compelling Conversations is a significant factor in increased school performance.

Conclusion

Compelling Conversations expand and elevate capacity within the entire professional learning community and contribute to sustained student achievement. Compelling Conversations are not merely a form of assessment, holistic accountability, and just-in-time professional development, though they are all that; they also establish new opportunities for communication through focused conversation that begins between the administrative team and teachers and proceeds to Data Teams. These meaningful conversations result in an intriguing network of interactions and relationships that work together in new ways to support student learning. Conversations are not "rolled out" like a new program. They are not instituted for political correctness. They are not a new buzzword. They do not have to be approved by the district office, nor do they require a line item in your budget. Instead, they connect ideas and people with students in a natural, personal way that is timeless. Through these conversations, transparency of information is crafted.

Conversations begin with one person.

You.

They are focused—one conversation with one teacher about one child.

One.

This is not a revolution.

I have questioned why the presence of the administrative team contributes so significantly to Compelling Conversations outcomes. With our home adjoining the Harpers Ferry National Park, answers await William and me in our walks. Reading historical plaques interspersed throughout the battlefield, I mused once again: Why did the presence of President Lincoln, standing directly at this location, contribute to the outcome of the Civil War? After all, the troops were in capable hands. Yet, the Commander in Chief made it his priority to travel the challenging route to be physically present at the point where decisions were being made.

Boots on the ground.

Education's "Inconvenient Truth" is we cannot defer to future generations the urgent actions needed or ignore the potential we have to impact lives.

No message is stronger than the statement made by a leader putting his or her boots directly on the ground where life-changing decisions are being made. This remains so today.

Here is education's "inconvenient truth": Just as our generation cannot defer to future generations the urgent actions needed to deflect the devastating effects of global warming, we cannot continue to overlook or ignore the potential we as leaders have to impact lives. As a contributing leader, consider traveling to that place where a year in the life of a child's progress is being determined. Honor the lives of those students under your watch by establishing conversations with their teachers. Through conversation, the promise of each student's potential may be released, forever contributing to the outcome of their future.

Glossary

above   A student receiving instruction that is above his or her enrolled grade level standards by one year.

administrative team   A leadership team composed of the principal, assistant principal, and others (could include specialists) who meet with each teacher for a Compelling Conversation.

aspiring leader   A teacher who has established the professional goal of becoming an education leader.

backward design   Beginning with the end in mind and designing toward that end.

backward mapping   The process used to establish the end goal and then determine achievable support goals that align with the end goal.

below   A student receiving instruction that is not at (*on*) his or her enrolled grade level standards.

Compelling Conversations   A process for holding regularly scheduled dialogues between each teacher and the administrative team to discuss student progress and acquire teacher-generated data for Data Team goals; also, the name for these conversations. Purposes of Compelling Conversations include: (1) understanding where all students are achieving, (2) taking a closer look at every student's achievement to establish goals, and (3) finding students *before* they are lost. Student progress is frequently monitored, both during each grade and *between* grade levels.

conditional knowledge   Knowledge, skills, or strategies that can be successfully transferred under different conditions in a new setting.

contributing leader   A principal or leader who contributes actively and directly to students' learning. The involvement through which contributions are made begins with Compelling Conversations, between each teacher and the administrative team, that reach the heart of student progress and instructional decisions. This type of leader makes the shift from how much the leader knows (*instructional leader*) to how to increase students' knowledge and understanding (how much students know).

core belief   The tenet that every child who leaves elementary school performing successfully on his or her enrolled grade level has a better chance for a successful, happy life.

Data Team   A team composed of teachers from each grade level and a Data Team leader, who meet monthly or at each marking period to establish student goals based on achievement data.

decile   The values of a variable that divide the frequency distribution into 10 equal-frequency groups. The ninth decile is the value in which 90 percent of the norming group lies.

double-instructed reading (DIR)   A structured reading program, for any children who are struggling with reading, that provides reading support for children *directly in their classrooms.*

Essential Questions   Questions that stimulate inquiry, debate, and further questions that can be reexamined over time.

holistic accountability   An accountability system that includes not only academic achievement scores, but also specific information on curriculum, teaching practices, and leadership practices; includes a balance of qualitative and quantitative indicators.

instructional level   The level at which the student can make progress in a subject (e.g., reading) with instructional guidance. This level has been referred to as the *teaching level* because the material to be taught must be challenging but not too difficult. Reading "on an instructional level" indicates that the student is learning and is able to transfer that learning with understanding. An instructional level is an indication of student performance that must be assessed with data from group discussions, student work, and formal and informal assessments.

Invisible Excellence   An outcome, *planned* for in September, whereby students make more than one year's progress in one school year, even though they may still not achieve grade-level standards. Invisible excellence occurs whenever teachers believe in their students.

on   A student receiving instruction that is at his or her enrolled grade level standards.

professional learning community A group of educators with a culture and orientation based on the idea that the core mission of formal education is to ensure that students learn.

root cause The deepest underlying cause of a symptom or symptoms, which, if removed, would result in elimination or reduction of the symptom(s).

slope of achievement The visual representation of achievement data on a line graph. Data, such as state assessment results, are plotted at yearly intervals. These yearly results become data points, which yield a line graph when connected. The results in an improving school would be represented as an upward inclination in the slope of the line.

standards The knowledge that students are expected to learn.

struggling readers Students who are not yet reading with comprehension at the grade-level standard.

tipping point The name given to the moment at which substantial change occurs all at once (Gladwell, 2002).

triangulation A process of gathering multiple data sets to focus understanding of an issue, rather than relying on a single form of evidence.

vertical team A team composed of teachers from each grade level and special area.

zone of proximal development A range in which a child can perform a task only with the help of a more experienced individual (Vygotsky, 1978).

References

Barth, R. (2002). The culture builder. *Educational Leadership, 59*(8), 6–11.

Bernhardt, V. (2002). *The school portfolio toolkit.* Larchmont, NY: Eye on Education.

Black, P., & Wiliam, D. (1998). Assessment and classroom learning. *Assessment in Education, 5*(1), 7–74.

Byrk, A., & Schneider, B. (2002). *Trust in schools.* New York: Russell Sage Foundation.

Carroll, L. (1865). *Alice's adventures in wonderland.* New York: Random House.

Center for Performance Assessment (now The Leadership and Learning Center). (2006). *Data Teams* (seminar and training manual).

Center for Performance Assessment (now The Leadership and Learning Center). (2004). *Data-driven decision making* (seminar).

CIERA. (2001). Put Reading First initiative. Washington, DC: National Institute for Literacy & National Institute of Child Health and Human Development, U.S. Department of Education.

Costa, A. (1991). *Developing minds.* Alexandria, VA: ASCD.

Costa, A., & Kallick, B. (2000). *Activating and engaging habits of mind.* Alexandria, VA: ASCD.

Covey, S. (2004). *The 8th habit.* New York: Simon and Schuster.

Covey, S. (1994). *First things first.* New York: Simon and Schuster.

Csikszentmihalyi, M. (1997). *Finding flow.* New York: Basic Books.

DuFour, R. (2002). The learning centered principal. *Journal of the Association for Supervision and Curriculum Development, 59*(8), 12–15.

DuFour, R., DuFour, R., Eaker, R., & Karhanek, G. (2004). *Whatever it takes: How professional learning communities respond when kids don't learn.* Bloomington, IN: National Educational Service.

Durkin, D. (1993). *Teaching them to read* (6th ed.). Boston: Allyn & Bacon.

Eaker, R., DuFour, R., & Dufour, R. (2002). *Getting started.* Bloomington, IN: National Education Service.

Fullen, M. (2001). *Leading change.* San Francisco: Jossey-Bass.

Garmston, J., & Wellman, R. (1999). *The adaptive school: A sourcebook for developing collaborative groups.* Norwood, MA: Christopher-Gordon.

Gladwell, M. (2005). *Blink.* Boston: Little, Brown.

Gladwell, M. (2002). *The tipping point.* Boston: Little, Brown.

Hargreaves, A. (2006). *Sustainable leadership.* San Francisco: Jossey-Bass.

Hattiem, J. A. (1992). Measuring the effects of schooling. *Australian Journal of Education, 36*(1), 5–13.

Lambert, L. (2003). *Leadership capacity.* Alexandria, VA: ASCD.

Langer, J. (2002). *Effective literacy instruction: Building successful reading and writing programs.* Urbana, IL: National Council of Teachers of English.

Lezotte, L., & McKee, K. (2002). *Assembly required: A continuous school improvement system.* Okemos, MI: Effective Schools Products, Ltd.

Lieberman, A., & Wood, D. (2001). *The work of the National Writing Project: Social practices in a network context.* Palo Alto, CA: The Carnegie Foundation.

Lipsey, M., & Wilson, D. (1993). The efficacy of psychological, educational, and behavioral treatment: Confirmation from meta-analysis. *American Psychologist, 48*(12), 1118–1209.

Marzano, R. (2006). The importance of building students' academic background knowledge. Presented at the annual conference of the Association for Supervision and Curriculum Development, Chicago, IL.

Marzano, R. (2003). *What works in schools: Translating research into action.* Alexandria, VA: ASCD.

Marzano, R. (2001). *A handbook for classroom instruction that works.* Alexandria, VA: ASCD.

McTighe, J., & O'Conner, K. (2005). Seven practices for effective learning. *Educational Leadership, 63*(3), 10–17.

McTighe, J., & Thomas, R. (2003). Backward design for forward action. *Educational Leadership, 60*(5), 52–55.

McTighe, J., & Wiggins, G. (2004). *Understanding by design* (2nd ed.). Alexandria, VA: ASCD.

McTighe, J., & Wiggins, G. (1999). *Understanding by design.* Alexandria, VA: ASCD.

Palinscar, A., & Brown, A. (1984). Reciprocal teaching of comprehension. *Cognition and Instruction, 2,* 117–175.

Paris, S., Lipson, M., & Wixson, K. (1994). Becoming a strategic reader. In R. Ruddell, M. Ruddell, & H. Singer, eds., *Theoretical models and processes of reading* (pp. 788–810). Newark, DE: International Reading Association.

Paris, S., Wixon, K., & Palinscar, A. (1986). *Instructional approaches to reading comprehension.* Washington, DC: American Education Research Association.

Perkins, D. (2002). *King Arthur's round table.* New York: John Wiley & Sons.

Piercy, T. (2003). Collaborative pacing conferences: The golden key for team-based reading improvement. In *Journal of MASCD* [Special issue, "Analyzing Student Work"],17–22.

Piercy, T. (2000). *Habits of mind. Enhancing reading comprehension instruction through habits of mind.* Alexandria, VA: ASCD.

Public Education Network (PEN). (2004, January 30). What the media are missing in reporting test scores. *Public Education Network, 4.* Retrieved June 15, 2006, from PEN@PublicEducation.org.

Reeves, D. B. (2005). *On common ground: Putting it all together—Standards, assessment, and accountability in successful professional learning communities.* Bloomington, IN: National Educational Service.

Reeves, D. B. (2004). *Accountability for learning.* Alexandria, VA: ASCD.

Reeves, D. B. (2002). *The daily disciplines of leadership.* Alexandria, VA: ASCD.

Reynolds, D., & Teddlie, C. (with Hopkins, D., & Stringfield, S.). (2000). Linking school effectiveness and school improvement. In C. Teddlie & D. Reynolds (Eds.), *The international handbook of school effectiveness research* (pp. 206–231). New York: Falmer Press.

Robbins, P., & Alvy, H. (2004). *The new principal's fieldbook.* Alexandria, VA: ASCD.

Routman, R. (2005). *Writing essentials.* Portsmouth, NH: Heinemann.

Routman, R. (2003). *Reading essentials.* Portsmouth, NH: Heinemann.

Routman, R. (2000). *Conversations.* Portsmouth, NH: Heinemann.

Schmoker, M. (2006). *Results now.* Alexandria, VA: ASCD.

Schmoker, M. (2002, June 24–29). Presentation at Harvard Principal's Academy. Cambridge, MA.

Schmoker, M. (2001). *The results fieldbook.* Alexandria, VA: ASCD.

Schmoker, M. (1999). *Results: The key to continuous school improvement.* Alexandria, VA: ASCD.

Schnorr, C., & Piercy, T. (2000). *Bringing to life a vision: Integrating and sustaining habits of mind.* Alexandria, VA: ASCD.

Senge, P. (1999). *The dance of change.* New York: Doubleday.

Smith, W. F. & Andrews, R. L. (1989). *Instructional leadership: How principals make a difference.* Alexandria, VA: ASCD.

Sparks, D. (2005). *On common ground.* Bloomington, IN: National Education Service.

Stahl, S. & Kapinus, B. (2001). *Word Power.* Washington, DC: NEA

Strecker, S., Roser, N., & Martinez, M. (1998). Toward understanding oral fluency. In T. Shanahan & F. Rodriquez-Brown (Eds.), *Forty-seventh yearbook of the National Reading Conference* (pp. 295–310). Chicago: National Reading Conference.

Tomlinson, C. and McTighe, J. (2006). Understanding by design and differentiated instruction: what's the connection and why should we care? Presented at the annual conference of the Association for Supervision and Curriculum Development, Chicago, IL.

Tomlinson, C., and McTighe, J. (2006). *Integrating Differentiated Instruction and Understanding by Design.* Alexandria, VA: ASCD.

Torgesen, J. (2004, November). U.S. Department of Education, No Child Left Behind. Paper presented at the "Reading First" Conference. Baltimore, MD.

Vygotsky, L. (1978). *Mind in society: The development of higher psychological processes.* Cambridge, MA: Harvard University Press.

Wenglinsky, H. (2004). Facts or critical thinking skills? What NAEP results say. *Educational Leadership, 62*(1), 32–35.

White, S. (2005). *Beyond the numbers.* Englewood, CO: Advanced Learning Press.

Wixon, K. (1986). Vocabulary instruction and children's comprehension of basal stories. *Reading Research Quarterly, 21*(3), 317–329.

Index